The
Tithe

The
Tithe
Challenge or Legalism?

Douglas W. Johnson

Creative Leadership Series
Lyle E. Schaller, Editor

Abingdon Press / Nashville

THE TITHE: CHALLENGE OR LEGALISM?

Copyright © 1984 by Abingdon Press

Library of Congress Cataloging in Publication Data

JOHNSON, DOUGLAS W., 1934-
    The tithe: challenge or legalism?
    (Creative leadership series)
    1. Tithes. 2. Christian giving. I. Title. II. Series.
BV772.J57   1984   248'.6   83-15890

ISBN 0-687-42127-6 (pbk.)

MANUFACTURED BY THE PARTHENON PRESS AT
NASHVILLE, TENNESSEE, UNITED STATES OF AMERICA

Dedicated to
Albert V. Hooke
and
Nordan C. Murphy

Foreword

"If you ask me, I don't believe we've overemphasized tithing and stewardship here," reflected a lay leader in one congregation, "but we sure get a lot of complaints about an excessive emphasis on money. A lot of our loyal members have responded to the challenge to be good stewards, but we've also created some alienation and a few have simply dropped out with the excuse that the church is only interested in their money."

"Ever since I came here three years ago, I've been preaching several times a year on the importance of the tithe," commented the pastor of another congregation, "and my preaching has begun to have some effect, but it sure is slow going."

"We've been thinking about a churchwide study emphasis on tithing as a way to get at our financial problems," observed an influential layman from a third church, "but so far we've not been able to find a good study book."

"In our church the word *stewardship* has been allowed to degenerate into a synonym for money," declared the chairperson of the stewardship committee in a fourth church. "We must do something to get us back to the biblical meaning of the tithe and stewardship, but I don't know where to begin."

This book has been written in response to the needs identified by these and similar comments that are heard in thousands of churches today.

There is a widespread need in the churches today for a serious study of giving. There are three reasons behind the emergence of this need. The most obvious is that the majority of congregations find themselves in a financial squeeze year after year. More important, however, is the fact that a study of the biblical basis for giving will change people's ideas and practices. Serious study is the best single approach for personal and spiritual growth in the area of stewardship.

The most subtle reason is we are repeating history. The churches have drifted into a legalistic approach to giving that parallels the conditions of five hundred years ago that sparked the Reformation in Europe. This time, however, instead of a reformation, the response tends to be alienation or apathy.

Five hundred years ago in Europe, the emphasis on legalisms and the apparent lack of any sense of the need for personal sacrifice by church leaders created the discontent that was a fertile seedbed for the Reformation. Today in North America, the Christian church is widely perceived as a voluntary association, and similar complaints tend to produce apathy or alienation or the quiet dropout. The best antidote for that condition is a systematic effort to reclaim our biblical heritage on the concept of the tithe. Douglas Johnson has given us a book that can help us reclaim that heritage.

Lyle E. Schaller
Yokefellow Institute
Richmond, Indiana

Preface

A study of giving is bound to change a person's ideas and practices. This seems to be the case no matter how many times one has previously studied giving. The demands of God are sharpened and life's responsibilities are put into sharp relief by such a study. At least that's the way things work with me. I hope the same might happen to you.

I have had the privilege of working with dedicated stewardship program developers and workers for a decade and a half. They will see their influence in this book. Nordan Murphy, through his friendship and dedication to stewardship, has done much to stimulate my thinking. Al Hooke, a friend and denominational stewardship leader, has pushed hard for me to complete this study. To both of them, I am grateful. While they influenced me greatly, I am responsible for the interpretations of giving and the tithe in this book.

Contents

The
Tithe

I

Old Testament Basis of Giving

The old man walked slowly into the room and laid his books on the desk. A professor of Old Testament, he looked as if he might have helped put the original script onto the animal skins. He cleared his throat before he spoke.

"The Old Testament is a collection of stories. It tells about a people who believed they were chosen of God to inhabit a land and to bring forth a new way of life.

"The Old Testament is a religious history. It shows how a group of people followed, strayed from, and came back to their faith over and over again. The history is full of broken promises, punishment, and rewards. It is a history written from a particular point of view. It tells how one group of people tried to be faithful to God in a world filled with temptation and greed.

"As you study the different books in it, look beyond the immediate events they describe and remember that the Old Testament is a message of the spirit. The stories are more about a God who is active in human life than about historical events. Read the Old Testament with this in mind, and you will know why I say it is a living book. After all, human greed, love, and emotions haven't changed that

15

much over time. The stories talk about people we know and current events."

The professor was more correct than most of his hearers realized. They considered the Old Testament a history of a particular people. Yet punishment in the form of an eye for an eye, rewards for the faithful, taking care and being accountable for what is entrusted to one, keeping one's word, and other such concepts form the basic morality that guides most of us daily. They are teachings found in the Old Testament. Indeed, the roots of human morality are found in stories collected in the Old Testament.

The Old Testament is a group of bittersweet stories about people who want to do the right thing. These people set rules to make certain they follow God's commands, only to end up breaking those rules and suffering predictable consequences. The stories also tell about God's devotion, anger, testing, and forgiveness of humankind. They make up a continuing tale about how God speaks and gives gifts to humans who accept those gifts, use them for selfish purposes, and turn their backs on the Giver. The content of the stories is about a people who call themselves Chosen, but their message is for God's creation no matter where they happen to live or what name they may choose to call themselves.

The Old Testament contains the basis upon which much of what we believe about tithing is built. The emphasis or understanding of tithing gotten often from the Old Testament is that it is a rule that must be obeyed. This rule supposedly was given by God to the writers of the Old Testament books. Unfortunately, people read the rule and ignore the spirit it is trying to convey. God didn't make up these laws; people did. They wanted to win God's favor; therefore, they set some strict standards for behavior.

A teacher and a student in an adult class were discussing

the nature of the Old Testament. They wanted to know its relevance for themselves and how it should affect their ideas about giving.

"The Old Testament tells us about God and how we are supposed to live."

"It doesn't sound like that to me. All the stories I hear are about somebody fighting somebody else."

"Well, there is a lot of fighting. I can't deny that. But there's a lot of loving and trust too. Remember the story of Isaac? He loved and trusted his father. And what about Noah? He trusted God and did what he was told. Then there was Moses. He was trusted by the people, and he trusted God."

"Yes. But the story of Joseph tells about his being sold into slavery. And Moses threw down his tablets and broke them."

"Nothing ever goes perfectly. People are worried about everyone else getting more than they have. They get jealous easily. And that starts fights."

"What is the Old Testament about if it isn't about fighting and wars?"

"It's about God's efforts to convince people that they need his guidance and love. It's about people like us who try to understand what God is and how he wants us to live with one another. It's really about giving."

Perhaps the teacher was being too simplistic, but the Old Testament stories *are* about giving, receiving, using, and giving back. Biblical scholars focus on the culture and location of the stories because they relate a history of a people. It's for that reason many people fail to see the relevance of the stories as a foundation for new concepts about tithing.

Suppose we were asked to put into one sentence the essence of the Old Testament. If we were faithful to our task, our sentence would have to focus on giving, setting up rules for receiving, using, and giving in return.[1]

This is not an effort to downplay the importance of the Old Testament as a religious history of a particular group of people. It's that too. The underlying theme, however, is greater than a culture or a particular group. It is a story of humankind. It shows how selfishness gets in the way of understanding and following God's intent. It lays foundations through rules and examples for good living and then illustrates how people ignore the rules so they may gain personally.

An understanding of the tithe begins with capturing the spirit of the Old Testament stories. Giving is the most important ingredient no matter what the story—creation, the establishment of a kingdom, Noah, the prophets, the captivities of the people and their return, or the Wisdom sayings and songs. In each story, God gives a person or a people something for their use and expects them to be faithful in the ways they use it, others, animals, money, and land. In the end, the glory of the use will be returned to God while people benefit from the gift and its use.

The message of the stories is giving, but just as important are people's rejection and misuse of the gifts. These must be part of the thinking about tithing so that it can become a living concept useful for modern life.

In this discussion, the aim is not to examine the religious history of a people but to discover what the stories say about how people should live together under God. The intent is to discover whether the tithe is a legalism—a rule that must be obeyed exactly in giving to the church—or a challenge—a minimum guide to giving rather than a prescribed amount.

It may be that the tithe, a tenth of income, is an inappropriate image for giving in the modern world. It may be that there is a new basis for giving which should take over from the tithe. It may be that the tithe is the most appropriate and best rule for giving regardless of the era. Perhaps or perhaps not. The challenge posed is to find an answer to the question, What is the tithe: a legalism or a challenge? Let's start with the tithe as a legalism.

The Tithe as a Legalism

A legalism is defined by *The Random House College Dictionary* as "strict adherence to law, especially to the letter rather than the spirit" of the law. This rather negative definition may not do justice to the tithe. After all, the tithe was a law developed by people living under God's jurisdiction. The definition may be too narrow to capture the import of what a tithe meant to Old Testament people. The tithe was a way of life for those people.

It may have been a way of life once, but, before becoming too defensive about the tithe, it is important to look closely at the implications of the word *legalism*. Once any connection between the tithe and legalism is examined, there is time to defend the tithe in more detail, if it needs defense.

A legalism occurs when the creativity and spirit that combined to make up the law are lost. Laws come about because people need guidance to solve their confrontations. Laws, when they are first written, have flexibility and "breathing room." Over time, however, the law becomes a legalism because those who are enforcing and interpreting it can't see beyond the words on a paper.

Laws are written to instruct, protect, and guide people. Legalisms are interpretations of those laws which take seriously only what the words say.

The preacher was waxing eloquent as he was reaching

19

the climax of the revival sermon. "Brothers and sisters, God has called us everyone to come to the healing side of Jesus! God said everyone! That means everyone! Now he was talking about the people down at the corner bar! And those sinners who are harloting around tonight! God help them! He was talking about everyone! Let's come on down here to the altar and talk to God about our souls! Come on down!"

An old woman rose and started, barely able to walk, to come to the altar. The preacher looked at her and said, "Sister, you have to know that God wants you, but the law he laid down won't let you into the kingdom. You can come and talk to God, but the law makes it impossible for you to enter the promised land with these other brothers and sisters." Her difficulty, according to the preacher, was the color of her skin.

That's a legalism. The preacher was talking about an interpretation of a law which sided with his beliefs. The law was for a historical situation and had nothing to do with this woman or her relationship with God. Unfortunately, laws that become legalisms are used to condemn and threaten rather than to encourage and guide. A law speaks to people about particular boundaries and obligations and privileges. A legalism is used to enforce a way of life that usually benefits those doing the enforcing.

Martin Luther King, Gandhi, and millions of others have objected to legalisms. They have stated with their lives that a law is made for people, not the reverse. They were willing to be charged with violation of unjust laws in order to change them. They sought to prove, and did prove at the cost of their own lives, that legalisms are inappropriate ways to guide the affairs of people.

Laws are important in governing the affairs of communities and people. Without laws, there is no structure to

20

group life. Chaos is a rapid and sure-fire result of having no laws. The Old Testament gives a lot of space to laws and how people are supposed to conduct themselves.

A careful reading of Exodus, Deuteronomy, and Leviticus shows how laws covered every aspect of life together including how the people should worship. The laws promoted a particular way of life. They were a practical shortcut to solving human relations among a nomadic people who believed themselves called by God to do something important.

"Laws are made to be broken." That cynicism expresses another reality about laws. Just because there are laws doesn't mean people are going to observe them. That certainly was Moses' experience.

Moses delivered God's laws to a chosen people, and the people ignored both Moses and the laws. Nor were the people interested in the spirit of the laws. Their attention was more pleasure-minded.

If laws were to be enforced and interpreted, it became obvious that there had to be a group of people especially assigned to do the enforcing and interpreting. That's where the priests came in. They were put in charge of interpreting and enforcing the laws. But it wasn't long before they lost the spirit of the laws, and the laws became legalisms.

Nestled among those laws were the first glimmers of what a tithe is and how much it should be of a person's income and wealth. These small references have stayed with us and have been taken over from those nomadic priests to be included in our modern thoughts about giving. As legalisms, at least, they have survived.

Three other concepts have survived as well. These are the idea of a person's being a steward (I Chron. 25–27), the bringing to God of the first fruits of a harvest (Prov. 3:9), and a time of forgiveness which should allow people to reclaim their property even though they are in debt for it (Lev. 25). These four ideas, including the tithe, have colored the thinking about giving. One can ask if the church is hampered by the legalisms of a past or whether those legalisms really do capture the spirit of what God is asking people to return to him and use in his name.

If the tithe is a legalism, giving becomes much like paying a bill. It is an obligation, and payment must be made. The letter of the law says the tithe is a tenth, which raises another issue. If it is a law, what is the proper base on which an individual is supposed to figure the tenth?

At this point, the tithe is a legalism. It denies the spirit of giving and rests upon a mathematical formula of compliance. When the tithe as a legalism becomes the foundation for giving, it misses the spirit of the law while being true to what the law states.

The tithe, when based on a spiritual interpretation of the Old Testament, is not a legalism. It cannot be reduced to a mathematical formula applied to income. The tithe of the Old Testament is a testimony to the interconnectedness of people and God. It incorporates a cycle of giving, receiving, and using. It signifies a relationship that can't be content with using a strict formula from the past. The tithe, like the message of the Old Testament, is a living witness to God.

Before turning to the New Testament and its interpretation of the tithe, it is important to examine the concepts of steward, tithe, first fruits, and jubilee. These are important conveyors of the notion that tithing is a spiritual experience based on a living relationship rather than the observance of a legalism. A living God does not rely on rules. God asks for giving based on the commitment. There is a significant difference between giving because of a legalism and giving because of being committed to God.

Steward

A steward is someone who manages or administers or cares for the property or affairs of someone else as an agent. The spiritual message of the Old Testament is that humankind act as stewards of God. This concept is first encountered in the creation story, which ends as humankind is given dominion over the earth and all that's in it (Gen. 1:26-30). Thus humans, from the very beginning, have been stewards of God's creation. That they haven't handled it too well is not the issue. The fact is that the Old Testament begins with God's giving, as a trust, creation to be in the charge of humans.

The Old Testament illustrates the idea of a steward in at least four cases, the first being in the story of Joseph. Joseph, after his ordeals of slavery and being a prisoner, is entrusted with planning and overseeing the crops of Egypt. He has a steward who does the day-to-day work of keeping track of what is being done with each part of the harvest, storage, and disbursement of grain. It is to this man that Joseph's brothers come asking for grain. The story shows how Joseph's steward is accountable to him, Joseph, as the keeper of Egypt's property (Gen. 44:1-5).

Three other descriptions of a steward are included in the Old Testament.[2] These expand and reinforce the idea that a steward manages something for someone else and is thus accountable to that person. There is one indication (Isa. 22:15 ff.) that some people can't be trusted to be good stewards; the power they wield as stewards gets them in trouble. Even that story, however, emphasizes that a steward is a person who manages an important trust for someone else and is wholly responsible for what happens to it.

The biblical basis for giving begins with God's giving

people care of creation. Humankind are God's stewards. Being a steward means people are responsible for how creation is used. The Old Testament is clear that a steward is responsible for caring for and using the creation to the benefit and glory of God, the creator or owner of the creation.

This is certainly a broad-based idea and one that cannot be contained by thinking only of money gifts. The whole of creation is not measurable by dollars and cents.

The second part of being a steward is accountability. The Old Testament spells out accountability mostly to apply to people working for rulers. It doesn't dwell much, except indirectly in the Psalms and the story of Ruth, for example, on being stewards of lives and of God's good gifts. In the Old Testament, therefore, a steward's accountability becomes a matter of obeying the law or agreements worked out between the steward and the master.

This notion that people are stewards of God's creation lays the foundation for New Testament treatments of what a steward does and the difference between a good and a bad steward. The idea of being a steward is important in the discussion of the tithe because of the breadth of what is being managed and for whom. All of creation is being managed for God. This is a mighty large order for those who believe a tithe is a tenth of what they might make. They forget the tithe might include time, talent, accumulated resources, the body, and the influence they have on others.

Tithe

The tithe is encountered early in the Old Testament (Gen. 28:22) and refers to an offering of a part of the spoils of war. In other references (Num. 18:26 ff., Deut. 14:22-26,

Deut. 14:28-29) it is an offering to God to ensure his continued good will. It is stated as a law in Leviticus 27:30. The tithe was not invented by current-day stewardship literature!

The tithe in the Old Testament was based on different social and economic systems from those of current times. References to the tithe in the Old Testament deal with fields, flocks, herds, and grains. In the Genesis reference, mention is made of people—slaves—being regarded as gifts. They had been captured in war and thus were part of the spoils of war. Tithing included giving one out of ten of one's newly captured slaves!

The last reference to tithe in the Old Testament, Malachi 3:8, is a prophetic illustration of how people rob God of tithes. In this instance, they do it by withholding their tithe.

The tithe was used to support the priests, generally the Levites. Their tasks were to fulfill the religious needs of the people as well as to uphold the law as recorded in the scriptures. They were not to own fields or to engage in agriculture. They were set apart for holy work early in the culture.

The assumption underlying the support of a priesthood which was unencumbered by work in the fields or vineyards was that they could regularly perform the rituals demanded by God. The people of the Old Testament believed that if these rituals were celebrated regularly and in the proper manner, God would continue to bless and support them. Keeping favor with God meant obeying the law. A part of that law was to give a tithe of what one received at harvest or at the annual roundup.

The practice of giving a tithe and the set-apart priesthood have both been passed down from the traditions of the Old Testament with few questions. A priesthood is important to every culture. In most, the priests are supported by gifts and offerings. The folk interpretation of these offerings is, "God will bless us if we praise him and give a part of our gain to his work." This is like a holy insurance policy. People want to be certain God knows their good intent and rewards them appropriately.

Some years ago a woman in a parish I was serving was dying. The phone call was urgent, and I hurried to the hospital as fast as possible. I arrived too late; she had died. Her daughter met me and said: "That's all right. You were here yesterday and had said the prayers and all. Today, just after I called you, I asked the sister to have a priest administer the last rites. It's a good thing Mom didn't know! She was a strong Protestant. But I figured that I ought to cover all the bases."

The tithe in the Old Testament is like a law to "cover all the bases." People are supposed to give a part of their earnings to ensure God's continued favor. A tenth is required according to the law. The spirit of giving which emphasizes gratitude seems to have been lost by this law which designates a specific amount to be given for God's work.

First Fruits

Those first strawberries of early summer seem always to be the best! They have had the benefits of nourishment from the winter and the slow warming of the spring. They appear in the garden full of flavor, juicy, and plump. The later ones don't measure up to those first few berries.

The first are the ones that should be given to God, according to the writer of Proverbs 3:9. In fact, the first fruits of all produce should be given to God's work (Num. 28:26 ff.) There is an ulterior motive in the admonition, however. The reason for giving those first fruits is to ensure good crops in the future. Honoring God so we can get good things in return is at least as old as Proverbs!

Honoring God with the best we have is what the writer in Proverbs was talking about. Praying in early morning, silent meditation before the bustle of the day, worship in the quiet of just waking are all forms of giving of the best to God. The writer in Proverbs was asking the reader to make a habit of giving the best.

Consider for a moment that the writer was not talking about giving to receive more in return. What if people gave of their best to honor God? Wouldn't they try harder to make next year's crops a little better? Isn't the advice something like what happens when an individual is awarded a first prize for some achievement? The person wants to try harder to be first again. In the meantime, the fields produce better than one could expect and the granaries are full. That's exactly what the writer suggested.

God expects people to give from the best they have. The first, be it fruits, efforts, waking moments, wages, belongs to God. In this instance, first means the best people have to offer. First fruits may assume the tithe, but the writer in Proverbs didn't mention how much should be given of what. The word was to give the first fruits. This may be much more than a tenth.

The idea of giving one's best efforts tends to qualify the tithe. A best effort in a race, for example, includes the entire race. A person can't be at his or her best for a tenth of the race and expect to win. Best effort is not limited. Why, then, is it acceptable to give a tenth of what we are and have to God? Is the tithe inappropriate when a consideration of first fruits is added to giving?

Some people would interpret the concept of first fruits differently. Their concern would be more literal and focus on material possessions. Even so, if God asks people to give of their best, it seems unlikely that God would limit the gifts or the striving to a tenth. This concept of first fruits must change the limitations of the tithe!

Jubilee

The twin concepts of sabbatical and jubilee are concerned with rest and restoration. The Old Testament says that land is to be rested every seven years so it can regain its vitality. God's creation, like God at creation, needs to rest and restore its energies.

This concern for restoration is the reason for having a year called jubilee. It came every half century. In Leviticus 25, jubilee, the time of restoration, was made into law. It applied to those who were property owners or who were in debt and had to sell themselves as servants to others. It was a powerful concept and property values, including the value of being indentured, were computed from the year of jubilee backward. It was like depreciating property today, only it was calculated from jubilee rather than from the date of purchase. The closer one got to jubilee, the less value the land or property had.

Jubilee is important to a discussion of the tithe because it emphasized God's continuing activity in the human situation. The spiritual message of the Old Testament emphasizes that God asks people to give not only to his work but to those around them. The chapter in Leviticus tells what to do about the property of those who had become destitute. They were to be given back the land which God had given them.

While one can be a steward of God, give a tithe of what is possessed, and give from the best of what is available, it is just as important to treat others as equal in God's eyes. Jubilee is beginning again, starting over with a clean slate as it were. The law gave the start-over a date, and people built an economic and legal structure around it. The spirit of the law is a concern for one another and sharing life's burdens.

Jubilee is a time of restoration, thinking about others, helping them get started once again. It is a time of considering what God wants people to do with their lives. As a concept of rededication, it supports the message and intent of the tithe.

The Basic Message

The spiritual message of the Old Testament is that people have been given creation as a trust, and they are expected to manage it for God. Whatever benefits they receive from the managing are theirs, but God expects stewards to tithe, to give from the best, and to observe a time when everyone is restored to the condition God gave them. People, in putting these expectations in force, made them laws which were to be enforced. Soon the spirit underlying the laws was gone, and rote acceptance and observance became the way of life for people.

Tithing was a way of life; this much is clear from the Old Testament. Being a steward, giving the first fruits, and observing jubilee are all a way of life. This suggests that treating the tithe as a legalism, a law without spirit, is inappropriate. It was a force in the lives of those people. It is true that people had to be reminded of the spirit of the law, but that's a function of prophets and interpreters of the law.

Observing the letter of a law can lull people into thinking they are special. The Old Testament kept telling the people that wasn't necessarily so. In God's way of doing things, it appears that observing the letter of the law can dull the senses to his spirit. That is the message of the prophets.

Their task was to keep calling the people back to God's side. The people kept the law but didn't feel the spirit behind it.

God wasn't pleased with this arrangement, and Jesus came. His message was "But I say unto you . . . ," an effort to instill in people an appreciation of the spirit behind the law. It is this blowing of the spirit that typifies the New Testament and is the next concern.

II

New Testament Interpretations

The New Testament brings to the laws of the Old Testament a new interpretation and an infusion of a new spirit through Jesus. His teachings, summarized in the Sermon on the Mount (Matt. 5–7), reinterpret the religious laws of Judaism. He invariably upholds the laws but gives them stronger requirements than did the priests of his day.

When it comes to giving, for example, he points to the widow who gave two copper coins as being more reflective of God's spirit than those who had more to give. He said that her small gift was greater than their larger tithes. In addition, he said that because she gave her money without fanfare and did not want to be noticed, God would more likely look upon her favorably. Through this illustration, Jesus pointed out that a void had been created by the way people observed the laws. He felt that priests and others required obedience without the spirit and understanding of God's intentions when the laws were given to humans.

To understand the power of the illustration, it is necessary to know the position of a widow in Jesus' day. A widow in New Testament times was at the mercy of her children. If they did not take care of her, and many of them

31

could not because they had to care for their own families in a poor agricultural economy, she was left to her own devices for staying alive. Jesus, in pointing to this widow, was illustrating giving as a way of life. He showed the disciples that obedience to a law was not enough. There had to be a new spirit underlying obedience to the law if they wanted to follow in the way of God.

This new way is the theme of the entire New Testament. Its stories and historical accounts illustrate what happens when giving because of the spirit of God becomes the basis of living. Jesus was careful to point out his obedience to the laws. He stressed that he was not replacing them but giving them new depth and meaning. This same feeling about the worth of the laws and the need to be obedient to them is found in Paul's writings. His conversion experience did not free him from the laws, but became a means for God to reveal the spirit underlying the laws.

Paul was persecuting Christians because he was trying to uphold the legalisms of his people. He was against Jesus until that day of conversion when he understood for the first time that Jesus was the personification of what the law was saying. Paul's conversion shows how God intervenes in life and what happens because of that intervention. The story shows that a person's life, once he or she meets God, becomes one of giving until death overcomes the body.

Over and over in the New Testament, through parable and in Paul's practical instructions through letters, efforts are made to breathe new life into the law. There is little evidence of anyone's trying to overthrow the law. Even when Jesus is confronted with picking food to eat on the Sabbath, he responds by citing the example of King David. If King David could do it, then it certainly must be acceptable for other people who must stay alive to pick and eat food.

32

Paying debts to Caesar was not overlooked. Indeed, Jesus said people had civil obligations which must be met. However, civil obligations are nowhere near as demanding as the requirements God puts on people. Jesus recites many laws in his teaching but, when questioned about the most important laws, says that the only laws God really cares about are to put God first and to love others as one loves oneself. These two laws, according to Jesus' way of thinking, summarized everything the law and the prophets had said (Matt. 22:37-40).

Jesus was not trying to replace the law with something new; he was asking people to look beyond it to see what the words meant, not what they said. That's the reason the focus of this chapter can be the phrase, "But I say unto you . . . " (Matt. 5:17-20).

Listening but Not Hearing

Many human failings are talked about in the New Testament, but the one which is most serious is not paying attention to what is being said. Jesus used parables to draw pictures for the disciples and other listeners. Even then they had trouble understanding. Listening but not hearing the spiritual demands was a failing Jesus often despaired of but which followed him to the tomb. It was a continuation of a human situation which had been faced in the Old Testament.

The people following Moses did not understand the difference between law and spirit. They kept straying from the way he had led them. The same thing was happening to Jesus. The people heard what they wanted but didn't understand the real message. For instance, Jesus told those he healed that they should thank God. He also told them to go to the priests and be declared whole and clean according to the religious laws of the day. He was trying to show that humans live through the grace of God's spirit even though they are bound by the community religious laws. They heard about the community but not about God.

The difference between a law and a legalism was discussed in chapter 1. Jesus illustrated that difference in his life. As an abider by the law, he sought only to make it refreshing and useful instead of harsh and unyielding. His reward for trying to emphasize the spirit rather than the letter of the law was a cross. That doesn't seem like an appropriate reward for a person whose message is a spiritual law.

This same theme of teaching the spirit and finding rejection among those whose life was given to interpreting the law happened to Peter, Paul, and the disciples, the tax collector, and to others in the New Testament. It seems that those who profit from legalisms are not receptive to others who try to make the laws come alive with new meaning. It is a tale told often in history, but for the Christian it finds the most vivid telling in the life of Jesus.

The message of the New Testament is that listening and following the spirit of the law are more important than learning and following the letter of the law. The message had the power to change history. The spirit of the law became a powerful force. However, observing laws and ignoring the spirit underlying them is more comfortable for most people. People hear but don't comprehend. That's the reason for Paul's letters. He had to keep explaining and interpreting. The spirit seemed to elude those who wanted to be faithful to Jesus' message.

This attitude shouldn't be surprising. It is easier to obey a law than be willing to get at the spirit behind it. A law is clear and demands minimums. The spirit of a law requires a maximum. For example, an eye for an eye is clear punishment for a particular violence. It is a minimum to pay for a very serious crime. Compare that to going a second mile or turning the other cheek to a person who has wronged you. These are maximum punishments because they require more of an individual than loss of an eye. In addition, to a law person, these punishments appear to be invitations for more and perhaps greater violence. Such an interpretation of the law asks for much more than most people are willing to give.

But giving as God has given is the heart of the New Testament. Over and over again the admonition of Jesus is not to be bound by laws or convention in forgiving or giving. He talks about a revolution of the heart and adopting a new lifestyle. He is saddened by those with many material possessions because their allegiance cannot be to God nor can they understand giving as a life pattern. That's the reason it will be hard for a rich man to enter the kingdom of God.

In the same way that Jesus turned the interpretation of the law upside down, his message changed the meanings of the concepts of steward, tithe, first fruits, and jubilee. If they were used at all, they were not regarded as legalisms but took on new meaning and significance.

The Tithe as Required

The Old Testament assumes the tithe as an appropriate gift to the rulers, especially when the spoils of war were divided. When the Levites, as a group, were designated to be the priests, the tithe was used to support them. While the nominal amount was 10 percent, some evidence suggests that for a few of the priests, the take was considerably higher.[1] Regardless of the unusual circumstances of a few, most of the people were expected to give a tenth of what they received.

Evidently the tithe was assumed by Jesus to be as legitimate as any other law. He did not mention the tithe as a requirement, but his teachings did not undercut any existing religious law. Since he supported all the laws, it is assumed that he supported the tithe as a law. His regard for the law is shown clearly in the Sermon on the Mount (especially Matt. 5:17-19). Being a lawbreaker was not for Jesus. He was a part of the chosen people and felt it a duty and a privilege to obey the laws they believed God had given them.

On the other hand, Jesus felt that the tithe, as practiced in his day, was not enough. He was particularly critical of those whose gifts were given as a display (Matt. 23:23). He emphasized that while the tithe was required, it was not enough. His feeling on this subject is given through the story of the rich young man (Mark 10:17-31). The subsequent discussion with the disciples shows Jesus' position.

Although a supporter of the law, he was not taken in by observance or display of observing any of the laws. His teachings suggest that he felt the law was the least common denominator. A true giver showed thanks not only to God but to others before the gift made any difference either to God or to the giver. His story of the tax collector (Luke 18:9-14) is evidence of his strong feeling about getting the spirit rather than merely observing the letter of the law.

The New Testament books, other than the Gospels, talk about gifts and offerings rather than focusing on a tithe. Paul (I Cor. 16:1-4) talks about giving as one prospers rather than being required to give a certain amount. It may be that his suggestions were made because he was dealing with Gentiles, whose history did not include the tithe. Whatever the reason, his interest was in being generous and giving without a measure.

The instruction for giving, for the support of the saints or apostles, comes at the end of a letter which emphasizes the need to uphold and go beyond the law. Paul takes the law of the Old Testament as a given but does not cite the tithe as one of those laws. When it comes to giving, he discusses it as something more than a particular percentage. He speaks of giving as one is blessed and carries this emphasis further in II Corinthians, especially in chapter 9.

It appears that the tithe, as a law, is not the necessity it was in the Old Testament. Jesus put a new stamp on giving; one gives out of gratitude to God. When this is the rule, the spirit of giving is based on a different set of circumstances than in the Old Testament. In addition, the New Testament is a universal message no longer confined to the Jews. Because of this shift in focus, the new law is emphasized rather than the old.

There are other differences between the New and Old Testaments affecting the teaching of the tithe. The first difference is that there is no professional priesthood to support. Those needing support were a limited number, the disciples and apostles. The need for money and gifts shifts from caring for the priests to making certain that the traveling preachers are cared for and that these itinerants have money to distribute to the poor. Without an organized group which depended on the gifts of believers, contributions of the faithful in the New Testament went to feed the hungry, clothe the poor, and care for the widows and orphans.[2]

The second difference was in Jesus' emphasis upon taking care of one's neighbor. The ministry of Jesus focused on creating human groups that cared for one another. Each person was responsible for the other. They could not pay someone else to perform services because of the command of Jesus that they should do for others as they did for themselves.

This meant that Christian discipleship was a personal ministry performed by a committed group. The groups were connected with each other by the traveling preachers and expressed their oneness through sharing. The sharing was not limited to the tithe but became an expression of their concern for others.

The third difference was that Jesus asked his followers to do more than the law required. Jesus wanted them to catch the spirit of the law and forget the legalisms. For example, when he fed the five thousand, he asked for all that was available, not a portion. This was an illustration of his ministry. If one is to follow Jesus, the demand is for total, not partial, commitment. This affected every aspect of life, including giving. With such an outlook, the tithe was no longer an applicable law for the New Testament.

Steward

The duties and position of a steward were evidently common knowledge to Jesus. In Luke (Luke 12:42, 48; 16:2-8), he uses examples of stewards to bring home the point that people are stewards of God's creation. While the illustrations show poor stewardship, the discussions following them clarify that Jesus is talking about people's relationship with God.

A part of his discussion is the need to be faithful with whatever one has, be it much or little. Faithfulness and being a good steward are measured not by content or accumulation but by attitude and understanding of God's commands. The inadequate stewards were those who forgot who was in control. They overstepped their authority and did not remember where that authority came from or that it required them to be accountable. Thus the steward in Jesus' stories and parables is everyone.

Jesus lives and teaches faithfulness to the law, but the law is not a legalism. It is a guide which illuminates the way in which people and God work together in God's creation. The steward is not a hireling but an individual to be trusted with oversight of the most precious possessions of the master. The covenant between master and servant is more than law; it is a mutual commitment. Each is accountable to the other.

The same message of trustworthiness and accountability for stewards is proclaimed by Paul in his writings. A steward is appointed to take care of things because he possesses the qualities of being honest and diligent in carrying out assigned duties. At the same time, Paul makes it clear that a steward is held accountable for what is left as a trust in his care (Rom. 14:12; I Cor. 4:2).

A steward in the New Testament is considered to be a co-worker with God. This concept is given by Jesus through his life and teachings and is promoted by Paul in his writings. Both assume the position to be useful to illustrate human responsibility and accountability to God for what is given for their use. The aim of the illustrations appears to be to get at the spirit underlying God's intent, and the obligations and privileges upon people who accept the use of creation.

Tithe

The few references to the tithe in the New Testament are illustrations of what not to do (Matt. 23:23; Luke 11:42; Luke 18:12). The tithe is not given positive reinforcement.

In fact, Jesus shows what happens when a good concept becomes nothing more than a law to be observed. He does not talk about it as a way of giving but assumes it to be a part of the law and therefore a part of life. This is what makes his illustrations effective; he is building upon something his seers and hearers recognize because they have witnessed it frequently. The admonition is that they might see the tithe given, but the spirit of how it is given and why it is contributed are much more important.

The tithe is not a part of the New Testament teachings either for Jesus or for Paul. Evidently neither felt it was an effective guide for giving. Their concern was much greater than the tithe. They wanted people to give more than the people thought they could. Paul's request was to give as they had been prospered or blessed. Jesus expected a lot more.

The tax collector, when he was confronted by Jesus, did not refer to a tenth as an adequate gift to those he might have wronged. His contribution to them was to be half of what he had. This way of expressing what God's mercy meant to him was far more generous and acceptable to Jesus.

The New Testament is a story of what happens when God's spirit is allowed to move in people's hearts. Jesus was able to lift them from the captivity of laws to a new assurance found in a relationship with God. When this happens, as it did time and time again in the records of the New Testament, depending on legalisms like the tithe is not appropriate. A new measure is necessary for faith and action. At the same time, a different way of looking at giving is introduced. It is because of this new way that Jesus and Paul did not consider the tithe worthy of their attention.

First Fruits

The idea of first fruits is taken up by Paul in Romans 8:23. The issue for Paul in this passage is that God has sacrificed the best for the creation. This is the same kind of message that is familiar from the Old Testament. The best or first goes to God, or in this case, comes from God to humans.

While Jesus did not mention first fruits, he kept before the disciples and listeners the message that God demands the best. Since the definition of first fruits used in this book is the best people have to offer, what Jesus sought was the first fruits of life from any who would follow him. The message of Matthew 8:21-22 is that the most important things in life belong to God. Human concerns, as they relate to social propriety and seemingly important obligations, are secondary to the call of God.

Jubilee

The idea of jubilee seems to have been lost by the time of the New Testament.[3] It was proving to be too impractical as a form of restitution. The number of people had increased, and the social structure was too formidable to try to keep it up. Anyway, it was only for the Jews and did not affect any of the other groups with whom the Jews might be involved.

The spirit of the jubilee, to remind people that they can have a new relationship with each other and with God, was demonstrated through the life and teaching of Jesus. He did not mention jubilee because it wasn't a practiced law or concept. Yet his message made some people want to help others get a new start in life. When he healed the sick and the lame, he insisted that they go to the Temple and the priests so they could observe the required days to show themselves clean and well. They were restored and used

41

the law to show others that they had been given a new
relationship both with God and with them.

The Basic Message

The New Testament is a group of books showing life
beyond the established religious law. It talks about a spirit,
a time for recognizing the great gifts given by God to people
and their responsibility and accountability for the use of
those gifts. It speaks of giving as people are able, not about
a law which requires everyone to give a tenth or a tithe to
support a group of priests.

The lives of people in those books display a form of
commitment which demanded nothing less than complete
sacrifice. The books also show the frailty of humans in their
desire to be like Jesus but their inability to follow through
on that desire much of the time.

The message of Jesus is captured in the phrase "You have
heard it said . . . but I say unto you." There are more
stringent requirements of believers who follow Jesus than a
mere law would suggest. It is a spirit similar to when God
came to Moses. The spirit and its requirements, as
described by Jesus, were not new. The newness was a man
who made people understand that it was the spirit rather
than the law that made the difference in life.

III

The Church and Giving

An inspiration from the spirit can last for a long time. The church testifies to that. But to refresh that spirit there must be a means to help people interact with God. For example, the disciples and apostles were spirit-filled people because they had been with people who had seen and heard Jesus themselves or had friends who had. They were in the "firsthand" generation. The accounts of life with Jesus were from those who knew.

Paul was able, in spite of not having seen Jesus, to feel the spirit because he heard firsthand accounts of life with Jesus. He talked with those he persecuted, the Christians. They had been with or seen Jesus. He became filled with the spirit as he tried to do away with them and their message.

God works in mysterious ways. Paul, the persecutor, became the chief architect of the church because Christ's message got to him. As a result, he became an advocate of Christ. If it had not been for Paul and his travels, it is likely that Christianity would have remained a sect of Judaism, with Jesus being regarded as one of the prophets.[1]

Support for the early church came from the believers.

Christians were asked to give as they felt blessed, as we saw in Paul's writing. Once the glow of Paul's ministry began to pass—almost as soon as he left town—a priesthood began to take control of the growing church. By the end of the first century, there is evidence of different offices of ministry. These were set up, and before long a standard procedure for administering the church evolved. The spirit was not lost, but it was being pushed into the background because of the necessities of making an institution viable.[2]

A system of taxes and tithes on the believers in order to support the clergy was begun soon after Paul. Voluntary giving was still used, but a priesthood demands a more systematic and regular means of support. However, not until Christianity had become the official religion of the empire did institutionalism and legalisms begin to replace the voluntary giving that characterized the more spirit-oriented earlier Christians.[3]

The subsequent history of the Christian church reveals the process used by those in power to assure the support of priests. Since they were priests, they had to be free of other duties to perform their tasks of preaching, teaching, and ministering to the poor and others in society. This movement toward a specialized priesthood changed the way in which people were asked for money and support for the church.

It is one thing to ask people who are filled with the spirit to give as they feel blessed. They respond with thanksgiving and are generous. It is a much different request to ask people to support a priesthood because the church is important and must be about God's work. The intimacy of personal religion is replaced by a professional who is trained to do what the church feels is important but which the individual may not deem necessary. The result may be a sense of reluctance and a deepening rebellion at giving freely to support the church.

This natural human tendency to resist authority seems to have been at work in the church of the Middle Ages. Not long after the church became a legal entity, about A.D. 323, state and community laws to assure support of clergy were needed.[4] It seems that free-will giving based on blessings had to be replaced by a more legalistic method. The Old Testament standard, the tithe, was resurrected to pay for the new order of priests.

An interesting parallel is evident between the reaction of people to Moses and to Jesus. Both came with words directly from God. Both were received for a while, and then their words from God were rejected. Finally the words they brought were accepted as the basis for belief and faith. When this happened, a priesthood was established to make certain that people were taught, that they obeyed, and that they were punished if they disobeyed the need for religious observances. At precisely this moment, a law was set up to ensure the support of the priests. This law was the tithe in both instances.

It was in the third century that the tithe began to be proposed as a standard for giving in the church.[5] The idea of giving first fruits was now looked upon as a practical method for giving. By A.D. 585, the tithe had been made the law of the church.[6]

In addition to legalisms regarding giving, the church became increasingly tied to the state. Beginning in A.D. 323, it increasingly became a state church. The means used to support the church changed somewhat because of the powers of the state. The change was that the state used taxation while the church used the tithe. For all practical purposes, the emphasis upon giving as one is blessed was replaced by legalisms. Giving was still important, but the means had changed. Raising money became a problem for the church and its members.[7]

The purchase of indulgences and the excessive financial burdens placed upon the faithful by the church in the Middle Ages became major ingredients in the combustible atmosphere that led up to the Reformation. The spirit of Jesus and those first Christians was lost by the Middle Ages.

Religion became not a living excitement but a crushing burden which squeezed the life and substance from the believers. The chronicle of the church's use and collection of money is not a happy tale.[8] The tithe is prominent in this story because of its misuse rather than because of its proper emphasis. This harks back to Jesus' citation of how not to give tithes.

The ideas of first fruits, steward, and jubilee were lost. They had come from a Jewish background, and their transference to gentile cultures was not made. The lack of emphasis put on personal responsibility and accountability caused these concepts to be lost. The spirit behind the laws was not evident during these times. As surely as church wed itself to state, the concept of giving changed from being an act of response to God's blessings to being a requirement of a legal system.

It was the dependence upon the tithe as a legal means of paying for the church that gave it somewhat of a bad name. The need for as much money as was requested never was acceptably explained to many people. The nonbelievers and non-Catholics were especially reluctant to pay for what they considered excesses of the clergy and the churches. It became more comfortable for everyone to have the state collect taxes for the support of the church. This was the situation at the time of the Reformation.

Reformation Through the Nineteenth Century

The various continental European reformations began because of financial reasons. Financial abuses were secondary to political motivations for the English, although there were many abuses.[9] While the reformers attacked the abuses of the systems for money collection and use of the pre-Reformation church, they did not emphasize the spirit of giving found in Jesus and Paul. Instead, they kept most of the money-collecting schemes, including the tithe, that were common.

Habits are hard to break, and laws are nearly impossible to repeal. While there were many abuses, state support of the church seemed even to the reformers to be a good way to ensure its continuation. Following the Reformation, after many of the financial extravangances had been attacked and reforms had been made, church and state were still very much intertwined. Most Lutheran states were unwilling to make a break in their support and control of the church. The same phenomenon occurred with the reformations in other nations and cities on the Continent, including Switzerland, and in England.

In areas of persecution and where nonconformists were located, the minority churches had to support their pastors through voluntary means. They could not depend on the state since they were going against the state in their worship. It might have been that they resorted to the tithe since it was a familiar form of support, but more likely they had other forms of raising money. Yet some nonconformists, when they became colonists in the New World, resorted to establishing a state church with it enforcing collection of money.[10] This was true of most of the first colonists.

The groups that were not a part of the state-church

47

background, Methodists and Baptists, most often asked for voluntary support for their ministers.[11] Since they had been existing on voluntary giving for some time, it was a continuation of their background. They weren't always very successful, but their intent was to make the church a reflection of its members. That meant the church must be supported by those who were moved by the spirit rather than the law.

From the beginning of the Christian church, through the establishment of colonies in America that advocated their own religious freedom, the concepts of steward, tithe, first fruits, and jubilee had either been lost or used as legalisms. The emphasis that these terms promoted, creation as a cooperative venture between humans and God, was lost in the institutionalism caused by the need to organize the church. The New Testament vision of individual responsibility and accountability had been replaced by the combination of church and state so that raising money was a form of taxation.

Change is a part of every organization, including the church. Eventually the various forms of enforced church support—taxes, tithes, pew rents, and the like—were abandoned.[12] In their stead, an emphasis grew to make offerings and gifts the main source of church support. In addition to these forms of money collection were endowments, bequests, and special collections. Most of the special collections and many of the bequests were for specific needs or programs such as missions. By the end of the nineteenth century, dependence on imposed funding mostly had given way to voluntary financial support. We need to examine briefly this history of change.

The first offerings in America, as they had been in the New Testament, were for the poor.[13] These collections were not frequent. The next need faced by colonial churches was to provide support for ministers' widows. This reflected a corporate responsibility that was shared among the churches of a denomination. The next step was to collect money to support the minister. At this early stage, such support became mostly voluntary, although money was secured in a variety of ways. The voluntary part of it was that not everyone was taxed and that no one told anyone how much to give.

An emphasis on stewardship and voluntary giving was made in the 1800s, but this was not long lasting.[14] An emphasis on the tithe, begun in the late 1800s, became an important part of church finances in the 1900s. The impetus behind the early tithe, and still a motivation, was that if a person set aside a percentage of money for the church, God would prosper that individual and the church.[15] This is hardly the motivation found in the early church, but it seemed to be effective.

Another kind of money-raising activity was the pew rent system. This was somewhat like the tithe except that it was a set fee for one's place at worship. It was phased out in most places by the end of the 1800s and was no longer used after World War I. When pew rents were abolished, the emphasis on nonvoluntary methods of collecting money to support the church, its program, and its minister was stopped.

This new dependence on voluntary giving did not shift the mood of the church members to contributing because they were filled with the spirit. Rather, the change in method of funding raised concerns about how to motivate people to give. Other forms of free-will type funding methods were used as well.[16] In each case, the method was to make giving seem less painful or, at least, less burdensome.

Voluntary support of the church had its problems. The

most important was the fear that some few members who gave a lot of money would want to control the congregation. This happened, of course, but the church survived in spite of the intents and efforts of a few people to make it a private chapel.

Meanwhile the concept of the tithe as a means of receiving God's blessing was promoted extensively. Its appearance in a congregation apparently was equated with finding a good method for receiving God's support. In a few instances, it was touted as the minimum level of giving, but this was not a universal emphasis.[17]

The concepts of first fruits and steward were taken up as efforts to motivate people to give more. The stress on giving in the 1800s was based on stewardship, for example. The idea of first fruits fit well in the agricultural economy of the early and mid-1800s. The idea of jubilee was not used. It had been lost, along with its message of restitution, centuries ago. A review of what is being done and has been done with giving and these concepts in this century is our next concern.

The Twentieth Century

Great changes in economy and world view have occurred in the twentieth century. The economy of the United States began as agricultural, changed to industrial, and then to being a producer and consumer of information by the last quarter of the century.[18] The century began with the United States as a sometimes-isolationist member of the world community with some interest in becoming a successor to Britain as a colonial giant. By the last quarter of the century, this attitude had changed because the United States found itself in a world economy over which no single nation could long hold control.

These changes in economy and outlook on the national and international levels were brought about by wars, depression, revolutions against conventions which had been prescribed through social and legal contracts, and a worldwide awareness of what it means to be an individual. Struggles against corporations and nations that deny personal worth have become commonplace. Insistence upon having freedom of choice in most things has changed thought and social patterns extensively.

The church, in its teachings about giving, has sought to keep pace with these changes. The primary difficulty of an institution like the church facing such huge changes is that it must retain its organizational structure and strengthen its requirements about ministerial training and placement while, at the same time, giving members choices in how, when, and with what they are going to support the church. Freedom of choice in support, especially regarding the amount, has produced great anxiety among some church leaders. This anxiety has been responsible for creating great interest in stewardship as a fund-raising activity.[19]

The variety of fund-raising activities has changed in form but not a lot in substance during the twentieth century when compared to the previous nineteen centuries of the church. The Lord's Acre or farm finds its roots in the Middle Ages as a form of support for the church and its ministry.[20]

The tithe has been around as a law for centuries. Twentieth-century books and pamphlets about the tithe have built on the Old Testament theme that if people give to God, God blesses them directly with worldly goods.[21] Other forms of fund raising have included lotteries, drawings, bingo, church socials, dinners, bazaars, and the like. They have their heritage in long-forgotten parishes of the early church.

51

Raising money for the church has been practiced for a long time; therefore, major innovations have been relatively few. Some types of fund raising might have been ignored for a while, but they showed up later as though they were invented for the first time. This was true of the Lord's Acre program, for example. The church farm was one of the techniques in the early Middle Ages for support of the ministry. The same is true of the bazaar and the church social, both important forms of raising money not only in the twentieth century but in centuries past.

The one innovation drawing upon the organizational skills developed by twentieth-century corporations is the every member canvass. This procedure incorporates planning and pledging, offshoots of corporate planning, and began sometime following World War II.[22] Since then it has become an accepted way of helping people determine the why of giving as well as how much they ought to give. The canvass, or every member visitation, process emphasizes church planning and insists on member involvement in program development and support. Where the canvass is used as it is designed, adequate support for the church's program has been reported.

As would be expected, the development of extensive and intensive stewardship programs has broadened the call for support from merely money to time, talents, and wills. A society that is encouraged to plan its life is asked by the church to include it in those plans. The need to include the church in one's life pattern is an important part of the every member canvass.

The four concepts traced in this book are parts of the stewardship emphasis in one way or another. A brief look at each of them provides a base for moving into the next part of the book, in which specific application of the concepts for lives today is discussed.

The tithe has been an important fund-raising technique throughout the century. The tithe's main theme has been that the giver receives rewards because of giving to God. The spirit of giving found in the New Testament has been downplayed. The tithe has been used because the church needs support. In fact, the tithe was started as a fund-raising method in the United States by congregations that were facing financial crises.[23] The congregations did not dwell on developing a spiritual life so much as they told their members that they felt God's church (their congregation) needed more money to survive.

The idea of steward has been difficult to deal with. Stewardship has generally meant raising money. The idea of being a co-creator with God, a steward of creation, has recently been reintroduced.[24] While this concern has been expressed by some people over the years, it has not been accepted as a major part of stewardship programs. If it was mentioned, it was in passing rather than as a serious part of the stewardship emphasis. The recent attention given to steward as co-creator is reminiscent of Jesus' life.

First fruits has been a useful concept for the rural and agricultural parts of the nation. It has not been helpful for the industrial and urban sectors which make up two-thirds of the populace. When first fruits is interpreted as giving the best one has to God, there is no limitation as to type of economy or job one is discussing. The concept affects all church members. This interpretation has not been used very much in stewardship literature or programs.

Jubilee, the restitution of property to others, has not been used since the Old Testament. Parallels to this concept are now showing up in the concern with wills and legacies. Some church programs ask persons to remember others, a form of the jubilee concern, as they make out wills and give money and property. Most of the will making, however, seems to focus on saving taxes. While endowments have a long history in the church, their concern has been for increasing the support of the church instead of caring for others.

IV

Giving in a Time of Affluence

"One of the things that puzzles me is why people don't give more to the church. People make a lot more than in the past, and the business pages of the newspapers say they are saving more. Why aren't they giving more?"

"They *are* giving more. The problem is that with inflation over these past few years, their giving just hasn't increased as much as they think it has."

"You've got a point there. They give a little more, but they make a lot more. We haven't helped them understand what giving in an affluent time should be."

This conversation between two denominational stewardship program developers suggests that people are willing to give to support the church's mission—and would probably give more if they were taught what giving means to a Christian in a time of affluence. The aim of this chapter is to help people understand what it means to give in a time of affluence. Also to be touched upon is the difficulty affluent people have with their attitudes about money and giving.

An Affluent Society

The United States ceased to be a nation of farmers early in the twentieth century. By 1920, more people lived in urban than nonurban areas. This trend continued, although it slowed after 1960, and approximately two-thirds of the nation in 1980 lived in major urban areas (counties with a city of at least 50,000 population). In spite of the trend since the early 1970s for an increasing number of people to move from urban to nonmetropolitan areas, the percentage of the population living in cities has not declined appreciably over the past thirty years.

People moved into cities because the economy changed. The United States had become an industrial society by the late nineteenth century. The industrial economy continued to increase through the first sixty years of the twentieth century. This was possible because improved farming methods made it possible to feed not only the people of the United States but many other people in the world with a fraction of the effort and investment of previous generations. The improvements in food production, industrial productivity, and union efforts to raise the income and status of workers made possible the growth of an affluent United States society.[1]

Many people in the United States who live in continuous want would dispute the statement that they are affluent. They would deny that their lives can be described as defined by *The Random House College Dictionary*, "conditioned by or based on prosperity or wealth." Yet these persons have access to funds and food supplies made available by the government or private charitable organizations that are determined that no one need be hungry or without clothes or shelter. These may not be the nicest or best kinds of food, clothing, or shelter, but they are available. Conditions in the United States are in sharp contrast to those in many nations of the world where lack of these basics contributes to a high daily death rate.

An economy, by its stress upon rewarding those who

work and who are shrewd, separates people according to the amount of money or goods they acquire. The Old Testament describes this separation process very well. The reactions of people to affluence or lack of it are illustrated by the story of Job.

The fact that the economic system during Old Testament times separated people into haves and have-nots was one of the reasons for introducing the year of jubilee. It was a time to reestablish an economic balance within the Jewish community. The balance was based on what they felt God had given to them as a nation when they got to what they called their promised land. The year of jubilee was a time when people no longer had to work as slaves or be indebted to one another. This concept was abandoned sometime after the Exile because administering it became too complicated.

In spite of inequities which exist in every economic system and will continue to plague humankind, the United States and some European nations as well as Japan are examples of affluence. Their people would like to have more than they have, but the basics of existence are available even to the most reluctant. A difficulty in living in an affluent society is that there are so many things one would like to have that the line between what is necessary and what is desirable is often obscured. A part of the reason for this blurring is sophisticated advertising.

Much media advertising makes things seem so important and easy to get that people are deceived into believing that they have a right to the things. Work and manipulation of monies in an economic system are ways to increase income and thus be able to buy more and more things. The basic right of a person in an affluent society is that of choosing to work at a job and then to accumulate enough money to buy what he or she can afford. Usually this will not be everything the person desires.

The need to work has been taken seriously in the United States and produced a mentality called the Protestant ethic.[2] The Protestant ethic made work a necessity and made possible the productivity essential to an industrial society. It was the bedrock upon which the factory system was built. This so-called ethic had roots in the discipline imposed on believers by many Protestant denominations that were founded in the United States.[3]

The Protestant ethic was misnamed. It is not Protestant in its origins; disciplined believers are as old as the Old Testament and certainly date in the church back to Paul's times. To call this discipline an ethic is to equate money-making work with Christian morality. In the Christian vocabulary, this stretches the definition of the word *ethic*.

Nevertheless, people have worked hard and have been rewarded for that effort by money, increasing amounts of money as the years progressed. They received money because the industrial system they worked in prospered. These individuals, through their disciplined work, made the industrial system affluent.

While people never think they have quite enough money, those who live in the United States are affluent. Many can buy what they need and have some money left to save. This is affluence. They don't have to worry about food, clothing, or shelter. Even if they get into too much debt to get out by themselves, there are legal remedies and they may start again with limited stigma.

Changes in the work patterns of the nation suggest even more affluence in the near future.[4] Perhaps the most significant change in this area has been the two-worker family. While this arrangement is not unusual in history, having two spouses rather than members of an extended family working is a different pattern than has been normal for the past century. This change has been profound during the past decade. During the 1970s, for example, the percentage of married women working at money jobs outside the home grew to more than half.

The major change brought about by two spouses working was that they chose to do so. They were not forced into the situation by need or by national emergencies. They wanted to work to achieve their own goals.

The result was that two-income families were no longer those with grown children who stayed at home and gave their earnings to the family. Nor were two-income families younger married couples with no children. Two-income families included those just getting started as well as those which were reconstituting a family after divorce, those in which women had been out of the nonhome job market for several years, and those in which two career persons married and each determined to pursue his or her chosen career.

The change from a single earner to at least two earners in a family has been significant for at least three reasons. First, the second income has been a family safety net. When one income has been cut off by choice—during a change of jobs or a personal readjustment period—or by force—a strike, layoff, or company relocation, the other income has generally been able to at least provide the basics. This has relieved suffering and want in many families that, in earlier times, would have had to depend on government or charitable support.

Second, the two incomes have given people more options. They have chosen to live in different accommodations or in a different part of the country. They have traveled or sent their children to private schools. They have

59

accumulated more material goods and luxuries. They have invested for their futures. These are options that are available to people of affluence, and two-income families help make the options a reality for many.

Third, two incomes have changed the expectations of families. The desire for personal fulfillment has grown as affluence has become more pronounced. Being able to realize personal ambitions means a family has to be free from want. Such freedom is available to more people now than previously because there are two incomes rather than a single income in a family. Now both partners can pursue their desires.

This is not to say that two-income families are blessed. They are faced with overspending, accumulating debts, and a feeling of being trapped in undesirable jobs and life patterns just as one-income families are. The two-income families are an important trend but are not any more of a blessing than one-income families.

While two-income families have become more common, single-income families have enjoyed the benefit of increased incomes as well. The average income of families has risen dramatically during the past two decades. Everyone, not just two-income families, has benefited. The entire society is affluent, not just a part of it. This has a direct bearing on giving since the concepts to be presented affect every church member and are not aimed at one group only.

Pressures of Affluence

"The good old days weren't so good. We worked twelve to fourteen hours a day just to put food on the table, clothes on our backs, and have a place to live. As I think back, I don't know what was good about it."

"I can tell you what was good about those days. We had a family. We cared about each other. We took care of each other. We did things together. We went to church."

"You're being too rosy, Judy. We had all those things but mostly out of necessity. We weren't any kinder or more loving then. We had to stick together, or we'd never have made it. None of us could do what we really wanted. We had to work all the time. Going to school more than the bare minimum was beyond us. A college education was a luxury."

"Al, you're just older than I am. College was something we expected. We knew it'd be hard to come by the money, but we went. What has surprised us is the change since we got out. Our world was smaller, and the expectations were limited. We thought little thoughts, and they were mighty conventional."

"That's the way it was with us, Jim. Jill and I both went to college, but we never expected her to work full time for more than a year or two before we had a family. It didn't work out like that at all. We both started working and liked it. Not only that, we got used to the two incomes and didn't see how we could get along with one. When the kids came, we made do for a while and then she went back to work. We aren't likely to ever be in a situation with only one working unless it's because of illness or something."

This is a cross section of a congregation discussing their lifetimes and what moneymaking means. They come at life from different perspectives because of how they have had to work. Beginning life with poverty as a constant companion conditions a person far differently than does a start with the expectation that education and freedom from want are normal. This latter expectation is more common among younger middle-aged adults in the 1980s.

Affluence makes a person's start in life easier in terms of

not worrying about basic human wants. However, affluence does more than alleviate worry. It has its own perspective and changes people's expectations over time.

In the case of Jill and Hank, their original expectations of a college education and both working for a short time fit into a model of their early adulthood. When they began living their model, they discovered they didn't like the restrictions. They did the natural thing; they changed their expectations. They enjoyed and wanted the benefits of affluence. As a result, they changed their life to incorporate two jobs and two incomes. They were not an unusual couple. They reflected what happened to many couples during the 1960s and 1970s.

Some couples can't live with the demands of two jobs. Vacation schedules often don't work out, caring for children and caring for home are not divided easily, and handling emergencies often becomes an emergency itself. More than one couple has opted out of two jobs/two incomes because they felt the demands were too great. This means they have made a choice in life which allows them the possibility of more time as a family unit and opportunities to do things together which wouldn't have been possible if both held jobs outside the home.

Another restriction of two-income families, besides less time to be together and to act as a family unit, is the pressure to do more or save more or both. Taking vacations to exotic places is a pressure felt by two-income families more often than by one-income families (if the one income is modest). Comparing notes on the job, talking about personal experiences, and giving each other subtle pressure to "keep up" happen in every work setting. When this pressure is applied to both partners in a family, each of whom is earning money, the discipline of saying no is harder to apply.

The same kind of pressure applies to accumulating things. A new television, video cassette, automobile, or home are some of the possessions increased affluence makes possible. More money also puts private colleges into the realm of possibility, and comparative notes on which schools children attend add pressures. Acquiring more because more money is available seems to be a human tendency.

While the discussion has been about two-income families, the same pressures and difficulties are present in one-income families. Increased income raises expectations no matter how low the income was before the increase. Pressure to accumulate attends an increase in available money.

Images of Want

A different kind of pressure on Christians is the cry for help, i.e., food, medicine, clothing, and housing, from millions of people in the world. The Christian is a world citizen, not a chosen tribe or a group confined to a particular land. The call of Christ goes to everyone regardless of condition, race, or place. It is not by chance that missionaries have gone everywhere with the story of Jesus and the promise of Christ. They have been compelled to be about the business of working with God to save humankind.

The pictures of hunger, death, degradation, and suffering have been transmitted to Christians through missionaries as well as news media. The message of giving, always present in Christianity, has been heard even when response has been minimal. Going into all the world and giving so that all the world might be free are twin concepts carried in the Christian message. This message has been transmitted to those in the United States as well as to those outside the nation.

The pressure applied by the images of want is hard to deal with. For many affluent people, these are pictures from unreal lands. It seems impossible that humans would be unable to find food or not be able to purchase the necessities of life. It seems equally unreasonable that the governments of these people would allow them to die of starvation and disease in a world which is so advanced that space travel is normal.

Giving money to help is regarded as an easy way out by some Christians. These are the individuals who want to give more. They agree to spend a year or more in service as a missionary within or outside the nation. They are of every trade and profession and of most ages. Their giving, as they have heard the cry of want, has been to stop their regular existence and help others in a firsthand way.

Volunteering one's time outside one's community or church is not possible for most Christians. They are tied to their jobs and their places of residence. In order to share what they have with others, they must give money. It is not a cop-out for them to send a check; rather, it is their own means of showing concern. This is the way most of us must express our Christian conviction.

The question most often asked in an affluent society is, How much should I give? It is an inappropriate question. The need of a Christian is to understand what giving is and then be willing to base his or her life upon the answer.

A Christian's question is not, How much of my life should I give to Jesus? but, When shall I give my life to Jesus? The first assumes a part, while the latter meets Jesus' request to give one's entire life into God's hands.

Jesus' trouble with affluence is apparent in Matthew's account of the rich young man (Matt. 19:16-24). This story shows the subtle effects of affluence. A person gets used to possessions and luxuries. Not only is it nice not to have to worry about where the next meal comes from; it is a pleasure to have two cars, a good savings account, pension benefits, and good clothes. It is easy to accumulate things because they can be purchased with credit cards and paid for once a month with little need for worry about next month's bills. It is the attitude as well as the practice Jesus was talking about.

His illustration of the widow giving copper coins points to attitudes as well. It is hard for an affluent person to understand need and want. It is difficult for an affluent person to be willing to sacrifice. It is almost impossible for a affluent person to imagine not being able to earn enough to buy food. The fact that people have to sleep on the street because they don't have homes is beyond reason for an affluent person. Even when an affluent person visits a place where many families spend their entire lives living in doorways or in alleys, he or she cannot believe this is done out of necessity.

It is hard for affluent people to get into God's kingdom because often they don't know how to give. The affluent life is based on accomplishment or being provided for by relatives or government. Affluent people think giving is providing people an incentive to do for themselves. Their lives are not based on giving. It isn't that they're so selfish; it's just that they haven't heard what Jesus said about giving. Even if they have heard, they haven't understood.

Giving in an affluent society demands a new attitude about one's life and responsibilities. Giving as a life pattern must be learned; it is antithetical to humankind, in whom struggle to meet basic needs has been a hallmark throughout history. Giving depends upon a person's hearing of Jesus' admonitions and an understanding that those cries of want are not from images but from people. The concepts of steward, tithe, first fruits, and jubilee are essential ingredients to every person who lives in an affluent society and wants to make being Christian a life pattern.

Steward

Giving in a time of affluence calls for a new understanding of steward. The concept was clear to Jesus; it meant someone who was in charge of another's possessions. The individual was a hireling, an employee. A parallel in current usage might be the person who is a manager in a company or a trustee in a church or a trust officer in a bank. These positions are responsible and demand accountability. Yet none of them includes the sense of intimacy and trust implied by the word *steward* in earlier usage. They are jobs, not ways of life.

In a Christian sense, a steward is one with whom God entrusts creation. Jesus showed that God didn't start things and leave. God works with humankind in making creation function. God and humankind are partners in creation. But even that image doesn't do justice to what Jesus described as God's relation to humans.

The image that best describes a Christian's relationship to God, according to Jesus' life and teachings, is as a member of a family. Being a part of a family is to be trusted and accepted but also requires responsibility and accountability. In a family, everyone works together to assure the welfare of everyone else. The talents of each person are essential as they work together as a family. They are a unit with a common purpose.

It is this spirit of unity of purpose between God and humans that best defines the word *steward*. A Christian steward is a co-creator with God. Instead of being a caretaker for someone who is absent, a steward works with God, who is present, to care for and improve creation. There is mutual responsibility and accountability. Together, God and humans are at work in the world to accomplish God's purposes.

The idea of humankind as co-creators with God suggests not that people living in affluence have more to use as they might want, but that they are asked to work with more than others have. The steward does not accumulate more and more goods and possessions. While this may happen, stewards are required to use wisely what is in their care. Stewards are responsible and accountable to God for those possessions.

The Christian who accepts Jesus' call to follow him and be a believer in God does so as a steward, a responsible member of God's family. The Christian becomes one of the people who are working with God in creation.

Giving in an affluent society demands that Christians become stewards of possessions. They are users of God's creation rather than possessors of it. They are required to give an accounting of how well they use those possessions, not how many they acquire. No longer can achievement be measured by how much one makes or has. The measure of a Christian is how well those possessions have been used in Jesus' name and for what purpose.

Tithe

In the same manner that steward required a new definition, the tithe must be understood in a new light. It is not a holy insurance policy or an investment in heaven. The tithe is a way of giving. Historically, the gift has been a tenth of one's income or gain. It has been measured in different ways over the centuries, but it still came out to be 10 percent.

Jesus did not ask for a tithe. He required complete dedication. A person who is serious about following Jesus must rethink what a tithe means for today.

First, the tithe is not an appropriate standard for giving in an affluent society. The tithe is a rather easy rule to follow and, by following it, the more stringent demands of giving are ignored. Too many people who give a tithe reason, "If I give a tenth, I am fulfilling my obligation to God." That's not accurate. The tithe has been imposed by priests in the Old Testament and the church in the New Testament. The tithe is not God's law. God's name has been used to legitimate the tithe.

Second, God's demands are far greater than the tithe, a 10 percent token of one's possessions. Jesus illustrated what those demands were by giving his life. The disciples and apostles followed those demands, and they paid what people in an affluent society would call high prices. Yet the demands of God are no different for people today than they were for those in the time of Jesus. The requirements are obedience to God and caring for those around us. If we can believe Jesus, the obligations of a Christian are to love God above all else and to love one's neighbor as oneself.

Third, the tithe, for an affluent Christian, holds no opportunity for sacrifice. No Christian through the centuries could truly witness to God's power and grace who did not have to sacrifice some material possessions. The tithe in an affluent society is no more than a charitable deduction. It doesn't help promote disciplined use of resources or a sacrificial approach to giving.

When the 10 percent standard is applied to Christians in an affluent society, it becomes apparent that a tithe is not enough. It may be considered a minimum upon which one can build a giving pattern.

Fourth, the tithe talks only about money. Giving should not be tied only to money. Jesus asked for the fullness of a life which means time, energy, and talent as well as money. These demands have not been diminished by the centuries. It is just harder for those with more time, money, energy, and talent to share with others.

First Fruits

It is difficult for a Christian living in a city or suburb to understand the image of first fruits. Interpretations have been made over the years, but they don't seem to help. Not many people in this affluent nation are close enough to raising things to understand the significance of giving the first produce for God's work.

Those who do understand the image know that there is something special about those first crops. In most cases, they represent the best that will be available. They have been cared for better than those that will come later. They have been harvested more carefully. And they are tastier than those that are yet to come. They are the best.

In order to use this concept in the discussion of giving, first fruits becomes equated with the best. We aren't talking about crops or any agricultural product. First fruits is the best a Christian has to offer. This includes the best time, the best talents, and the best part of his or her possessions. No matter what the item or commodity, God demands the best.

When we use the idea of first fruits as being the best that a person has, giving is rediscovered. Giving is no longer confined to donating the discards of life to the needy. Giving suddenly requires the best we have to be given for God's work. This makes giving not an exercise of little consequence but a time of great decisions.

There is another aspect of giving the best. If God asks for the best an individual has, it becomes important to that person to invest a part of himself or herself to make certain the gift is used. Giving one's best enforces the need to be a steward.

Jubilee

The year of jubilee, the time of restitution, has not been considered practical for centuries. Yet the need for a sense of equity and balance in possessions has not diminished. Each economic system emphasizes the haves at the expense of the have-nots. This difference is not to be overlooked, but there is a problem with it from the standpoint of a Christian. The Christian must know how to give so that some restitution can be made to those who have less primarily because they were born in a particular place to a specific situation.

Giving to others, the second great commandment, is a part of the concept of jubilee. Resting, returning, giving back are all elements of jubilee. Giving in in affluent society must include all of these if it is to be a meaningful and Christian experience. This giving can best be done through trusts and deferred giving or in wills. How one goes about giving after death is important to the concept of jubilee.

Giving in an affluent society, then, means that one gives of the best that is available from his or her possessions and income; cares for life and possessions as a co-creator with God; considers the tithe to be a minimum gift that includes time, talent, and energy as well as money; and considers the importance of jubilee or restitution when giving through a will. These concepts provide the basis for considering giving as a life pattern.

V

Giving as a Life Pattern

"You know, I've run into something I don't know how to deal with. I always thought that kids, once they got to be adults, would leave home and be on their own. That's what I kept telling my kids, but for some reason mine leave but they come back."

"I can sympathize with you but from another angle. I must be a soft touch because the kids come to me to help them get money to buy big-ticket items like a house and cars. They always pay up, but I could use the money for investing or buying things I have put off."

"It sure is good to know that other parents have the same problems with grown children that I do. I love them, but being hit up for money every month or two is getting old. I'd put a stop to it, but I don't have the heart. I remember what it was like to struggle and get along with nothing when we were young."

"As a parent with grown children who don't ask for help, I sometimes wonder what I did wrong. They're so independent they don't need me anymore. We taught them to take care of themselves, and they've done just that. Somehow I need to break this feeling that I have a continuing obligation to them."

These parents, in an informal way and focusing on their children, are discussing how to develop a life pattern that includes giving. They aren't verbalizing giving as a goal or a worthy motive. They are talking about a life pattern they began a long time ago and are wondering how it must be changed to deal with current circumstances.

A life pattern is the way a person structures his or her life. A life's structure is built on values he or she has developed. The values come from several sources, but the most permanent ones come from the family and the church. Values tend to be stable even though a person may stray far afield from time to time.[1] It is the stable value system that gives a person the basis for working at life's situations and problems.

A Christian's values are woven into the fabric of a life pattern the same as everyone else's. This doesn't happen just because an individual decides to be a Christian. Values create habits and ways of thinking. When a person becomes a follower of Jesus, the old or conflicting values must be changed. That's what is meant by conversion. The value system is changed.

Changing values is very difficult, as Jesus said many times when he was confronted with people who wanted to follow him. "Let the dead bury the dead . . ."; "I will make you fishers of men . . . "; "Give what you have . . . and follow me" are pleas to people who wanted to be disciples but found habits hard to break. Each time they couldn't break with the past, Jesus was sad but realistic. He knew the interest was there, but the discipline wasn't.

A few people were able to follow Jesus immediately. They just changed their lives, but even they had trouble with the habits. James and John got into an argument about who was going to be the greater in God's kingdom. Peter denied knowledge of Jesus because he was used to saving his own neck. Habits are hard to break, and some linger on no matter how strong the effort is to do away with them.

"But no one said it was going to be easy." How many times have we heard and said that? Jesus was candid about being a follower of his. "You won't have any place to call your own, not even a bed" (based on Matt. 10). That's a drastic future, but it was his warning to all who would be followers. He was telling them and us that a believer's life pattern was far different from the accustomed way.

Those who have grown up in the church or in families that have had a strong relationship with the church often feel that their habits aren't in need of change. They have practiced Jesus' commands since they were children. No one needs to tell them what a giving life pattern is. They know! Perhaps this is the case for a few. Most people, however, are like the young man who asked Jesus what more he had to do to inherit eternal life (Matt. 19:16-22). He had kept the major commandments since he was small, but the one he lacked—and couldn't make himself accept and keep—was giving away some of his possessions.

Many church people are like the young man. They have kept Jesus' most obvious commandments and have values that enforce their desire to be like Jesus. However, they are unable to change their habits about money and possessions. They still feel that what they have is theirs to use as they see fit.

No wonder the most difficult change in habits for Christians living in affluent societies revolves around money and possessions. These Christians have been taught that what they earn is theirs to keep. They have difficulty with any concept that suggests that God is the owner and humankind are the users and custodians of creation and all that is within it.

The life pattern of John Wesley, as it dealt with money, was captured in the admonition to earn all you can, save all you can, and give all you can.[2] Most Christians in the United States can relate to the first two parts of that statement but get off the train just before the last stop. They haven't put giving, at least as Jesus taught it, into their functioning life pattern.

This is strange because the church through the centuries has taught that giving and sharing are expressions of Christ's presence in one's life. Stewardship writings have emphasized giving as a requirement, a discipline, for a Christian. On every side, the Christian is reminded of the value system that motivated Jesus. The symbolism of the Cross suggests that continued giving might not be appreciated by everyone, but that giving is the way one discovers God.

Giving as a life pattern means the idea and practice of giving must be etched into a Christian's habits. This is something like making a little memory chip for a calculator or computer. Once the pattern is entered, it becomes "burned" into the chip and cannot be removed. To remove it, the chip must be replaced. For most Christians, the giving memory chip is slightly toasted and not burned. Because of this, quick and easy formulas for giving are used rather than the giving requirements of Jesus.

It's time that the old giving memory chip is removed and a new one is burned into place. This new one must be based on Jesus' blueprint and put in place through conviction. It will have to include the concepts of steward, tithe, first fruits, and jubilee as they are interpreted in this age. Without such pathways of thinking about giving, the concept of giving as a life pattern might never be implanted.

Some False Assumptions

Giving is a habit just as not giving is a habit. The amount and kind of gift given are determined by assumptions about the needs of a church, people, missions, and one's own ability to give. These assumptions are usually based on pieces of experience and information gotten through the church or someone else. A few common assumptions influencing giving are false.

1. *I will give what's left.* There is nothing left. Everything is used, be it time, energy, talent, or money. When giving is based on unused excesses, there is no giving. There might be some contributions, but this is like throwing crumbs to the birds in winter. This kind of giving is not worthy of a Christian. A Christian doesn't give leftovers to God.

2. *I don't need a budget.* Budgets are essential to everyone. Young people with allowances must plan how they are going to use their money as well as how they might earn more. Individuals must allocate their resources so they have food to eat, clothes to wear, and a place to sleep. Families must plan to meet expenses for medicine, transportation, recreation, and schooling. No one is exempt from planning expenditures. This is budgeting no matter how informal it might be. A Christian makes certain that the budget includes giving as a high priority.

3. *I will give as the spirit moves me.* Giving is a discipline, not just a few random contributions generated by emotional highs. A life rooted in Christian values is disciplined. It moves toward a goal and follows a purpose. Unless a person is disciplined in every part of life—including giving—there will be no discernible pattern and few worthwhile contributions from that life.

4. *I will give to service organizations and not to the church.* There are times when the leadership of a church does

things that people don't like and can't agree with. That's the problem with human organizations; they aren't perfect and often don't do the things they say they are doing. But only the church has consistently been able to right itself and move back onto course through the centuries. It alone has been the long-term champion of God's creation. Even in its imperfection, it tells the story of Jesus through people's lives. It is the focus of a Christian's giving.

Components of a Giving Life Pattern

The concepts of steward, tithe, first fruits, and jubilee have been examined and interpreted at several points in this book. It is obvious that they are important. However, they are visible expressions, not the foundations of a giving life pattern. Such a pattern must be based on a solid foundation since it means a change in the way people live. The four concepts mentioned above are expressions of a change in life values. This change happens when a person's life becomes founded upon four components.

The four components upon which a giving life pattern must be based are study, discipline, prayer, and action. A brief discussion of these components is our next concern after which we will discuss the four concepts of steward, tithe, first fruits, and jubilee. A life pattern based on a solid foundation will emerge from these eight elements.

1. *Study.* A person can't read the Gospel stories of Jesus without being impressed with his knowledge both of the scriptures and of the religious laws of his people. One of the more interesting of these stories is the episode when he was discovered missing a day after his parents had started from Jerusalem on the way home. They found him discussing the law with the priests at the Temple.

This story about Jesus indicates that one of the

components of a life pattern similar to his requires knowledge. When one studies, as he must have, the study should have two focuses. The first is to learn about the scriptures, the religious law, and the church. Note that the word *study*, when applied to Jesus, means reading, thinking, and discussing. It does not mean accepting without question, giving back only what has been read or heard, and arguing. Jesus amazed the priests because he thought after he read. Paul did the same, and so did many other church leaders through the centuries.

Study means learning the message of the scriptures, not memorizing and reciting scripture verses. Study involves using various resources, including teachers, to help understand what the scriptures say. God gave people minds to reason and think with. Study focuses attention and effort on a topic. When applied to giving, it deals with how one's life pattern can be based on giving and discovering God's directions.

A second direction in study is to hear, see, and feel what others are saying and doing. Jesus was very sensitive to the needs and wishes of people. He knew them because he had observed and listened to their inner needs. Not many people are willing to do that nowadays. They are interested in talking about themselves and their hopes but are short on patience when other people want to tell about their own needs.

Study, from the perspective of Jesus, includes both book learning with reasoning and people learning with listening and observation. A Christian whose life pattern is based on giving will study the scriptures and read the history of the church while reasoning out God's message from the stories. At the same time, the Christian will learn to listen and hear God speaking through others.

2. *Discipline.* Jesus' life is a study in discipline. He did not

77

change his pattern even at the end. He was captured because the priests knew where he would be—praying in the garden. Another example of his discipline is in the story of the temptations in Matthew 4. During these temptations, he did not waver from his determination to be obedient to God.

Discipline is based on a conviction that what one is doing needs to be done and is correct. Sometimes discipline requires lonely perseverance, while at other times it is supported by others. The giving life pattern must be based on discipline. The discipline needed includes budgeting, decisions about what portion of one's income and possessions should be given to God's work, and acting on the decisions. Discipline always includes action after study.

3. *Prayer.* It is impossible for a Christian to live without regular contact with God through prayer. Prayer is not always for confessing or for asking God for something. Prayer for a Christian includes listening. Listening occurs as one stills the mind and heart to catch the message of God. This message might come as a small voice within, or it might come through nature, or it might come from another person. Prayer is an attitude of receptiveness to God's message.

The giving life pattern depends upon prayer. No one can be a steward or understand giving without being in constant touch with God. Giving and sharing are not natural for people; these attitudes have to be learned. Prayer is an important part of the learning process. It is also necessary as a way of making oneself sensitive enough to listen to those in need.

4. *Action.* Giving, above all, requires action. It is possible to study, pray, and be disciplined and still not act. The Christian life is full of action. It is based on doing, saying,

and being. Jesus, for example, was always moving, teaching, and healing. Paul never stopped going from church to church. No less is required of any believer today.

Not many are called to travel to exotic lands or be great preachers. We are asked to act in Jesus' name wherever we happen to live. There are disheartened, discouraged, hungry, and ill persons around our homes. The Christ of the New Testament says that the Christian's responsibility is to minister to them. If one professes to be a Christian, it becomes his or her responsibility to act toward others in Jesus' way and name.

These four components are basic elements for a Christian who intends to develop a giving life pattern. Making a decision to move into such a pattern will take study not only of the scriptures but of one's present life patterns. Such personal study will try to find ways to change existing habits so that new ones can be developed which support a giving life pattern. In addition, study is required to discover how the pattern of giving might best be implemented.

Discipline is required to keep attention and effort directed on the giving life pattern. It is easy to slip into comfortable habits and ways of life that are counter-productive to giving. As people, most of us are more willing to receive than to give. It takes discipline to reverse that kind of negative willingness.

Prayer for grace and discipline is a continuous part of a giving life pattern. No one can begin or maintain a giving life pattern without God's presence. Jesus couldn't, so why should we expect we can?

Unless we implement—put into action—a giving life pattern, all of our study, prayer, and discipline will be wasted. We have to live the pattern before it becomes a reality. It is not enough to talk about it, study how to do it,

79

pray for help, and be disciplined. To be giving means that one gives. Christians are active persons, always proclaiming through their lives that Christ makes a difference in the world. If we believe it, we have to live it.

Expressions of a Giving Life Pattern

In the part of the Midwest where I spent my first years, there was a phrase we used to show skepticism. It was, "I'm from Missouri. Show me; don't tell me." It wasn't that no one was believed. The phrase reflected an understanding of human nature. People there knew it's a lot easier to talk than to do.

When it comes to giving, it's much easier to talk and think of reasons for not giving than it is to set a life straight and give. That's one of the reasons it's relatively easy to tithe in an affluent society. "If you're only talking about a tenth, we can swing that. I thought you were talking about big money," one person responded to the idea of the tithe. If a Christian is serious about giving, it means living by a different set of values relating to money and its use than is common.

Values can't be seen. People don't know one another's values except as the values are expressed in the way they live. Paul put this well in his description of love in the first letter to the church in Corinth (I Cor. 13). Values—in Paul's letter the main one was love—are expressed by the way a person behaves.

While some people try to fool others by acting as if their motives are based on love, Paul said that in the long run only those who truly love will be able to continue that life pattern. Eventually it is the strength of the values, that is, how well people base their lives on the four foundation components, that determines the long-term effect of a giving life pattern.

The four external or observable expressions of a giving life pattern are being a steward, giving of one's best (first fruits), the tithe, and jubilee. The next chapter will deal with jubilee. Attention now is directed to the other three expressions of a giving life pattern.

1. *Steward*. Most people never will be rich. Most people will consider themselves not worth much in material possessions. Most people will feel that they don't qualify to be stewards. They don't have enough.

Everyone has the same amount of time, but each person uses it differently. Everyone has some skill or ability that can be useful to another. Everyone has feelings and the possibility of loving and being loved. Everyone can come in contact with other people. Everyone has an environment, a part of the earth, over which he or she has some control. The amount each person has of any of these is limited by situation, place of birth, and other factors over which he or she has little say, but the fact is that these are possessions just as surely as are money, clothes, cars, and places to live. Everyone can be a steward whether he or she wants to acknowledge it or not.

A steward treats creation as a co-maker. No matter how much or little of that creation is given to his or her care, the steward treats it as a part of him or her. Being faithful with a little is as important as being faithful with a lot. A businessman once told me, "If we find out that an employee has cheated by a dollar on an expense account, we fire that employee. We feel that the amount is not the issue but the fact that the person cheated at all." That's a hard attitude, but it reflects the company's feeling about being a steward. An employee is responsible and accountable and must take being a steward very seriously.

81

If this is the attitude of a commercial company, isn't the message just as tough for those who call themselves Christian? They have been told what is expected of them. They know God is a co-worker in life. Jesus told them the two great commandments. It should come as no surprise that a Christian is a steward. But the Christian is a steward with a specific aim in life. That aim is to be like Jesus, and it means developing a giving life pattern.

Such a life pattern, as a steward, means that the amount or type of possessions one has is not the issue. At stake is how every possession is used and for what purpose. There is no rule that says one cannot increase the possessions or try to earn more. Neither is there a rule that says a person can't be content with what he or she has. A steward uses whatever he or she has and possesses to the glory of God and helps make life better for others. The main themes of a steward are to do nothing that denies God and to do everything as if it were being done to oneself.

2. *First fruits.* Goodwill Industries began and continues as a self-help project for those with disabilities. It has been able to provide jobs for people who would be otherwise unemployed. A part of the reason for its success is that churches have helped collect discards of all types from their members. It makes no difference if the item is in disrepair; the persons at Goodwill Industries will fix it and then put it up for sale. The aim of helping people with little hope for productive lives has worked well.

Unfortunately, the attitude that people give only those things they don't want or need to others has become a generally accepted form of giving. In this study of giving and the tithe, it has become increasingly clear that God asks for the best and first rather than castoffs and what's left. This is exactly the opposite of what Goodwill Industries asks for. What a difference it would make if they asked for the best! Such a shift turns giving upside down. The gift has to come from those things we want and find desirable for ourselves. Giving in this way is a sacrifice.

Think about the shift in values that giving the best we have requires! It means that if we teach church school, we have to prepare the lessons during those times when we are most creative, not at the end of the day or week when we are tired and preparation is a burden. It means that the money we give to the church comes out of the check first before any obligations or savings are even considered. It means that we must take an inventory of our skills and volunteer them to the church or to benefit other people. Giving the best becomes a serious business.

It is impossible to believe that a giving life pattern that emphasizes contributing the best one has to God's work can be done without study, prayer, discipline, and action. God works in mysterious ways, but it is up to people to be in touch with God to know what their part is in the way God wants them to go. Regular contact with God is essential when people are interested in giving their best to God.

3. *Tithe.* The tithe can be a legalism, or it can be a challenge. The material presented previously has shown how the idea of a percentage of income (or spoils from war) became a standard for giving. This standard was used to support an institution and pay priests both in the Old Testament and in the history of the church. In each case, the tithe was collected by law, not by voluntary action. As such, it became a legalism—a law that lacked spirit.

The tithe was rediscovered in the last part of the nineteenth century and was used as a means of strengthening the financial support of congregations. The idea caught hold, and tithing spread. One of the difficulties of this spread was the feeling that God rewarded people because they gave a tenth of their income to the church. What seemed not to impress people was that God was present whether or not they gave anything to the church. God's grace is not limited to tithers.

Yet stories about personal success once a person started to tithe were spread about and made tithing seem attractive. Everyone would like God's help in becoming financially successful. It is not God's way, according to Jesus, to pick people and make them financially secure because they tithe. It is much more likely that the mechanics of tithing, such as the need for financial planning, more careful study of options of how to use money effectively, a disciplined approach to money, and acting decisively after plans have been made were the primary contributors to tithers' success. Merely giving a tithe does not ensure God's favor, according to Jesus.

Tithing, however, can be a challenge. In an affluent society, people need to relearn the message that giving is expected of a Christian. Not many give a tenth,[3] but, if they did, the work of the church could be fantastic. For those interested in developing a giving life pattern, the tithe can be a first step in creating new habits. It will not be enough, and focusing only on money tithing is insufficient. But considering the tithe as a start, a challenge, is a creative way of establishing a new life pattern.

Combining the concepts of steward, first fruits, and the tithe becomes exciting. A steward is aware that everything one has is to be used for God's work. If the steward gives a tenth of the best as a beginning habit in developing a giving life pattern, the work of God will be strengthened beyond belief. That tenth can be given through the church, or it can be directed to help people in other ways so long as those ways emphasize love and care for others.

At no point does a giving life pattern involve violence,

deceit, death, or political revolution. Jesus' example shows that the giving life pattern is to be lived among people in whatever condition they may be found.

It is time now to outline a process through which the giving life pattern might be developed. The elements have been traced through history and interpreted for current usage. The foundations underlying a giving life pattern have been discussed. It is necessary to create an application procedure to incorporate them into a viable pattern we can use in our lives.

Creating a Giving Life Pattern

"You know, Pastor, you can talk about doing things like love and all that, but we need some directions. We're practical people. We like to have things spelled out for us."

"But I go on the assumption that people can apply what I say without my trying to give directions. What I would say probably won't do any good for most people."

"I am sorry to have to disagree, but I do. We need directions as a primer to thinking. We're not dumb or anything. It's just easier to get the drift of what we might do when somebody takes the time to tell us how to do it. We probably won't do it as you want us to, but we need your help."

The pastor laughed. "What you're asking is for me to go the next step. I don't usually do that for the public; I think of applications for my own life. That might be a good discipline."

The pastor and this layperson point out a need we all feel. People need ideas that challenge them to consider what they might do differently with their lives. However, people need also to have some trail markings or a way to incorporate that challenge into their lives. They need practical guidelines for putting ideas into action.

One of the responsibilities of leaders is to discipline themselves to go the second mile. They must present challenging ideas to stimulate people, but then they must help people meet the challenge. Leaders should give the followers specific ways for making challenging ideas become a part of their lives.

Many books on stewardship are available which provide guidelines for individual giving.[4] They talk about pledging, wills, stewardship, and proportionate giving. In addition, programs are available which, if followed, help people with financial planning, proportionate giving, will making, and understanding the implications of being a steward.[5] A review of one or more of these will be helpful to a person who wants to create a giving life pattern.

Citing other references, however, does not relieve me of the discipline of providing guidelines for developing a giving life pattern. The following suggestions, therefore, are given to assist you in your studying, reasoning, praying, and disciplining as you create your giving life pattern.

Step 1. *Study your present life pattern.* Pay particular attention to how it affects your attitudes and actions in giving. Be certain to include more than money in your analysis.

Review your checkbook records for the past six months, get a diary and chart your time use (what you do and for how long, including such things as transportation, family time, volunteer activities, education, and so forth) for two weeks, and list ways you have used your skills and talents during the past month (noting when this use has been for personal benefit and when it has been to help others).

These lists are historical data that tell you the ways in which your present life pattern channels your energies.

These data give you an accurate picture of your life pattern because how you spend money and use time reflect your basic values. The review of where money went alerts a person to what is most important in life. For example, if half the monthly income is spent on shelter or transportation, it becomes clear that this is a most significant part of life. If, on the other hand, a third is spent on entertainment, one can begin to wonder whether this is because of boredom, a search for meaning and purpose, or a means of escape.

Each person, after collecting these data, must interpret the figures into a life pattern. However, discovering what percentage of the money went where and for what, no matter how small the total amount of money available, provides clues about the present life pattern. The same kind of analysis and interpretation is necessary for use of time, skills, and talents. The composite of these interpretations is your current life pattern and reflects your basic values.

Step 2. *Study your current life situation.* Answering the following questions will help define your life situation. What are your responsibilities on the job, at home, in the church, and in the community? What are your expectations and ambitions? What do you want to accomplish with your life? Who depends on you and why?

Answers to these kinds of questions are necessary as you look for ways to modify your current life pattern. For example, if a person has a family of three young children and is a single parent, his or her situation and possible modifications would be different from those of an individual who just retired, has an adequate pension, grown children, a spouse in good health, and can be active if he or she chooses. Changes in life patterns are unique to each life.

Step 3. *Contrast your current life pattern with a giving life pattern.* The ideal contrast is with the life pattern of Jesus or a life pattern taken from the teachings of Paul. The contrast between one's current life pattern and a giving life pattern can help identify areas where change might be needed.

Step 4. *List changes that might be needed based on the contrast.* Take a piece of paper and draw a vertical line to divide it into two parts. On the left, list what you think are major components of your life pattern, define your current life situation, and describe how your pattern and situation affect your ideas about and practice of giving. On the right-hand side of the page, define in your own words the concepts outlined in this book: study, prayer, discipline, action, steward, first fruits, tithe, and jubilee. As you write your definitions, put down what changes are necessary in your current life pattern to make it a giving life pattern.

Step 5. *Develop a strategy to make the changes in your life pattern.* On another piece of paper, entitled "A Strategy for Creating a Giving Life Pattern," write down what you think you will need to do to get from where you are now to the giving life pattern. For some people, the suggestions might be extensive; for others, the list might be short.

Now is the time to put down how you can become a steward, what you will do to give of your best to God, and how the tithe will become a challenge in giving your money, time, skills, and talents to God's work. You need also to put down how you are going to use the rest of your life as a testimony to God's grace and love.

Step 6. *Take time to pray and listen.* After you have the data about your life and a strategy for changing it before you, take time away. Put it aside for a while and spend much time and effort in praying and listening. While prayer has accompanied each step of this process and will continue to be part of everyday existence, focusing it now is a helpful discipline. This sort of focus will be needed many times in the future when the temptation to shuck the whole process gets strong.

Step 7. *Calendar your proposed changes.* Get another piece of paper and write yourself a calendar. On this calendar, put down specific acts of giving that you want to accomplish by or on particular dates. For example, you might put a money gift of 10 percent of your income on the fifteenth of the month for the church. The calendar might include early morning prayer and devotions each day at the same time, such as 6:30 A.M. The calendar might include practice time for the choir you might join.

The calendar is your contract to put into action what you have decided. Up to this point you have studied, prayed, and disciplined yourself to develop a plan of action. This step is putting that plan to work.

Step 8. *Evaluate your progress regularly.* At least monthly return to your descriptions of how you might be a steward, a giver of your best, and how you understand the tithe as a minimum for giving. Review your actions by using data such as you collected in step 1 to see how closely you have come to making the changes you outlined in step 5. Adjust the way you are going about living so that you can come closer to your goal of a giving life pattern.

Creating a new life pattern is very difficult, and it takes the rest of a lifetime. Disappointment in your ability to stick with the new will be a companion. It will take a great amount of discipline and constant doses of resolve to follow the plan you design. Take heart; Jesus went this way before us and showed that it is possible. He didn't say it would be easy, nor did he say the rewards among people would be great. He said that you will see great things happen to people when you have a giving life pattern. What more could we ask than to see the hungry fed, the lame walk, the blind see, and those without shelter have a place to live?

VI

Giving Through Willing

"What's this about our church having a conference on making a will? How come our church is involved in that? That's not their business. They just can't leave people alone, not even after they're dead."

"It's not that at all, Helen. A Christian believes in life after death. Why should that apply only to a soul? Why not make what's left after we're gone work for the church the same as we do now? We ought to give our money an afterlife."

"That's ridiculous! I worked hard my whole life to make ends meet. What little there is when I die is going to my children, not that they need it. It's the principle of the thing."

"You don't have to shout. That's your decision to make. I'm going to the conference. I might learn something. Besides, it seems a shame to me not to make a continuing contribution to the church. My family ought to be able to make it without my help. At least that's the way we taught them."

A person with a giving life pattern is often confronted by individuals who think death is a time for making the family name and monetary success synonymous. These individuals might raise doubts in the mind of a Christian. The Christian then wonders why an individual shouldn't keep on witnessing to God's grace by giving to others and continuing to support the church after death. If a person's life doesn't stop at the grave, why should witnessing cease? These wonderments often are taken no further than thoughts. There is no easy way, they think, to make their witness except through the church. They forget the power of a will.

A will is a legal document through which an individual can give specific instructions about the distribution of personal effects and the body after death. A will is very important because it is the only document which can assure one that attention will be given to personal requests about how his or her possessions are to be divided. Even though a will is acknowledged to be important by church members, it is not made by many of them.[1] This is too bad because without a will, the survivors are powerless to continue the giving pattern of an individual.

When a person dies without having made a will, the state is empowered through the courts to determine how personal effects are to be distributed. To allow a court to decide how one's life possessions are to be divided is to negate a Christian's emphasis on giving. It is a perversion of a Christian's intent to witness to God to allow the state and the courts to distribute the possessions. Because a will allows a person to influence the world after he or she has died, it is sinful for life planning not to include giving after death.

Thinking about witnessing to God through a will is new territory for many church people. Over the years, endowments of money and land have been an important way of supporting the church. Indeed, church lands, because of endowments, had become extensive by the time of the Reformation.[2] The fact that people support the church through wills has been documented. At issue is whether this is the only way a giving life pattern should divide possessions.

A person with a giving life pattern ought not to allow giving to be limited or to stop because of death. Giving through a will ought to specify the way an estate is to be distributed, the way in which the body is to be disposed of, and the kind of memorials that might be acquired and dedicated. A Christian does not allow a giving life pattern to end suddenly because his or her heart stops beating. A giving life pattern extends through death to include a careful plan for distributing all earthly goods to others.

A Christian, whose entire life has been wrapped up in giving, will want to make as certain as possible that the pattern of helping others continues so long as he or she has any possessions. The possessions include money, one's body, and memories through documents, pictures, and recordings. It is up to the person whose life pattern is based on giving to write a will that plans for the careful distribution of these items so they can do the most good for the greatest number of people. A plan is the basis for the will.

Before going into procedures for developing the plan underlying a will, it is important to deal with four questions that have been asked about wills and a giving life pattern.

1. *If I give liberally throughout my life, what's left for me to give after I'm dead?* The assumption underlying this question is that disciplined givers will have spent most of their money during their lifetime. This is false. A disciplined giver is the kind of person who manages money well and, because of that, tends to have money and property left at death. Being a careful steward influences one to not be

guided by spur-of-the-moment decisions about money. It is the undisciplined giver, the person swayed by his or her emotions in the use of money, who spends resources by whim. Such an individual tends not to have any possessions remaining at death.

2. *What do I give in place of time, talents, and skills?* During a lifetime, an individual may have done a lot of volunteering. This stops when he or she dies. It is a fact that at death, personal time ends. This means that using skills and talents in face-to-face situations is not possible. However, not all of a person's skills and talents need to be buried. Some skills and talents, as well as personal influence, ought not to be lost at death.

For example, pictures, writings, recordings, and personal encouragements extend far beyond death. Separation through death is not so great when the person who dies has made a conscious effort to leave a part of his or her talents and skills for others to use and enjoy. This has happened in art, literature, science, and other areas of life. While not many of us will change the world by our discoveries or writings, each can influence and lighten the burden of another. Since this is possible, it becomes a responsibility of a person with a giving life pattern to make certain his or her skills and talents are given tangible form after death.

3. *Why shouldn't all of my possessions go to my family?* Many people believe they are helping their children by giving them money and possessions. This may be the case, but often a family becomes immersed in conflict as each surviving member tries to get more and more of a deceased person's money or possessions. It is important that a person's will continue the giving pattern of life at death and that the family's portion not allow any family member to become less disciplined in his or her life.

A person decides how hard he or she must work to accomplish personal goals. When an outside source, such as a gift through a will, meets some of those goals without any effort on the part of the individual, he or she might become complacent and greedy. A will based on a giving life pattern ought to be constructed as a challenge to survivors, not as a windfall which can become an invitation for them to be less disciplined.

A gift that challenges should be the aim of the will of a person with a giving life pattern. For example, one college with which I am familiar has a privately endowed loan fund which is part of its financial aid plan. Students may borrow money from this loan fund, which is financed through a will, for a limited time and at lower-than-market rates. The will of this donor left a challenge gift. Its use requires both the college and the students to be responsible and accountable. This kind of giving helps people immediately and requires them to develop discipline.

4. *Should I give only to the church?* Giving through a will ought to encourage and challenge people. If this can be accomplished by giving only to the church, it ought to be done. However, giving to the church so it will be a family or personal memorial is not appropriate.

Setting up endowments must be done carefully as well. Many congregations have been ruined by well-meaning members who left generous endowments. A congregation's current members must meet the annual challenge of financing their own mission. Giving that cuts out that challenge is not beneficial.

5. *Who should help me make decisions about my will?* A profession surrounding will making has developed over the past few years. The members of this profession are bankers, lawyers, financial consultants, and, in some cases, church advisers. They make it their business to know

legal requirements regarding estates and how to help survivors save tax money. Their work is important in a complex society.

It is a good idea to consult with some of these people from time to time. However, while it is good to know what these people think and to receive assistance in understanding the intricacies of tax laws, it is essential that an individual be in control of making the will. Decisions affecting giving throughout life have been made by the individual; and decisions about giving after death, as many as are appropriate, are the responsibility of the individual. A person with a giving life pattern does not allow someone else to take over this responsibility.

What to Give Through a Will

Equitable distribution of money and property is the goal of most wills. In some families, however, the will is used as a final act of spite rather than as a message of grace. When this happens, money and property become contested in court, and any semblance of care and concern for others which the writer of the will may have expressed in life is voided in death. The will of a person with a giving life pattern must be consistent with how that life was lived.

In order to provide some consistency between giving while alive and giving after death, a person needs to plan carefully what can be given through a will. The best way to handle the planning is to identify *what can be given before, at, and following death.*

More and more people are thinking about distributing some of their possessions while they're still alive. They are not being hasty or morbid but are trying to plan the distribution as carefully as they did the accumulation of possessions. For example, it makes sense to distribute family heirlooms before death so there will be fewer chances for conflict. Giving heirlooms, especially jewelry, china, silver, or possessions which a person will not use again, allows the giver and the receiver to enjoy their use rather than having the heirlooms remain in storage or on permanent display. Heirlooms can be given to individuals who appreciate their value to the donor.

Conversely, it is impossible to donate body parts until death. The donor must alert family members of the intention to give body parts since there are legal requirements that must be met. Also, an individual has no idea how long life will extend and must keep some money and possessions for use until death. These can be given through the will following death.

It is not uncommon for people to have difficulty thinking about death and wills. This extends to planning general funeral arrangements, such as deciding about burial or cremation and where the service will be held. Many people feel such thoughts are morbid or too frightening to deal with. No matter. Someone is going to have to work at it. It is much easier on survivors if a person makes specific requests and does planning before the event.

It is important to face death realistically and to discipline oneself to make out a giving list. It is a testimony of a giving life.

A giving list is a list of what one plans to give away. This list, prepared some time prior to death, ought to contain the following three parts (or, if you prefer, it may be three separate lists): (1) items to be given prior to death; (2) items to be given at death; and (3) items to be given following death.

The giving list may be constructed by sitting down from time to time rather than trying to get it done in a single session. This technique gives a person time to take a careful assessment of his or her probable needs during the last part of life. Such an assessment ought to be informed by conversations with doctors, financial consultants or bankers, family members, and friends. These people might give conflicting advice, but their suggestions can be weighed and balanced against one another. With such advice, useful decisions can be made.

Once decisions about what to give are made, a plan of action, that is, how to proceed with giving what to whom or for what purpose, can be written down. Then it becomes a matter of following through on the plan.

1. *Items to be given prior to death.* Growing old can be a time of increasing self-pity, or it can be a period when a person accepts the fact of death and prepares for it. Preparing for death is not giving up life and waiting for the end. Preparations are much more positive. They include deciding what is needed to make the remaining part of life comfortable and deciding how to dispose of unnecessary items.

One of the items that can be given is land or unneeded property. Ownership of land can be transferred with provision for keeping a part of the money from the profit or maintaining ownership of the home until after death. Cars and other vehicles can be given away or sold. If this is done, it will mean an increasing dependence on public transportation or the goodness of an individual for rides. Heirlooms and a portion of money can be given away or put into some sort of trust.

Giving things away while one is still alive cuts out much potential conflict. It also assures people of their part in any inheritance which will benefit them. In my experience, when this kind of giving is done well, everyone involved in the process is much happier.

It should be clear that this part of the list must be

conservative. A person never knows what the future might bring, especially older persons who are more susceptible to disease. An individual should not give away so much that personal independence and self-identity suffer if he or she is faced with a long-term emergency. This is one reason for getting advice before completing this part of the list. Giving before death is a discipline of careful planning and shouldn't be hindered by unwarranted fear or unrealistic optimism.

2. *Items to be given at death.* It is difficult for many people to even consider giving a part of their body to someone else. Yet God's world is based on giving and helping. A giving life pattern is one that wants to help others in whatever way is possible. This can be by donating a body organ to a living individual. A body organ donation may be agreed to by the person when he or she is still alive, or permission can be granted by written instructions from the survivors. A giving life pattern takes on consistency when the dead person helps someone to a fuller life through sharing a part of his or her body.

Approaching death is an appropriate time to decide how to share other kinds of gifts which a person hasn't felt free to give before. These might be a letter of appreciation for lifetime friendship and help, precious paintings and pictures, instructions to help a person over an especially difficult time in his or her life, and suggestions or guidelines for a loved one's understanding of death and life. A wise person would make decisions regarding these gifts and leave instructions with a responsible person to make certain the items are distributed at death.

Such gifts ought not to be sentimental ramblings—although there will be sentiment attached—but things to think about, times to remember, and hopes for the future. These can be very individual. They become a legacy for the future and challenge the recipient to live up to the hopes of the dead person.

3. *Items to be given following death.* This list should include everything that is not on the other two. Final disposition of material goods is the major import of this list. If the other two parts of the list were carefully drawn, this probably is the shortest of the three parts. It includes those things, including money, that were kept to assure the final years of life being wholesome.

The list that has been developed needs to be reviewed from time to time. The first part of the list may be spread over a few years with some of the items being given one year, some the next year, and so forth. It is not necessary to be hasty or to overload the giving process. One needs to be as disciplined in this giving as in every other aspect of giving.

Spreading giving over a few years allows a person to change his or her mind about what kinds of gifts to give to whom. It may be that some recipients—individuals or churches—cannot handle gifts. They may not be disciplined or responsible in their use of possessions, and the giver may decide to redirect further gifts to other recipients instead.

Spreading giving over time allows the giver to explain why certain kinds of gifts were or were not given to a particular person. These explanations can be done person to person instead of leaving someone wondering why. It is much easier to deal with misunderstandings between two live individuals than it is to try to offer rational explanations after death, when personal conversations between the giver and the recipient are impossible.

Giving as a life pattern is not easy. Making certain the pattern of giving continues after death is even more difficult. However, through a carefully drawn will, gifts can become a challenge to others rather than a crutch so they don't have to strive so hard.

To Whom Shall I Give?

Perhaps the most important decision when a person is drawing up a will is to identify the beneficiaries. The names of those to whom a sum may be payable are required on every insurance policy and many savings agreements. The amount and kind of possessions are important mostly because of to whom they are going at the individual's death.

The family is usually a primary beneficiary. This is spelled out in order of sequence, as, for example, spouse, children, and the next in line if none of these survive. It is not enough to say spouse. It is necessary to indicate exactly what is to go to whom. Usually the bulk of what is left is given to the family. However, a person with a giving life pattern will consider other people and institutions in the will.

An institution such as a hospital, fine arts museum or institute, college, university, seminary, or the like might be an appropriate beneficiary. The amount of money or possessions given may be small, but it can be meaningful so long as its use is left up to the receiving institution's directors.

The church is an obvious choice as a beneficiary of money or property through a will. It is helpful, in order to challenge the congregation to support its own ministry, to indicate a range of activities the grant can fund rather than allowing the money to be used as a financial buffer. A gift should not make life easier on a congregation. Money from a will should help a congregation improve or expand its ministry.

Finally, other persons who might be able to use the gift in a unique way ought to be found and included in a will. Such persons may be known to the donor, or an organization or a person can be authorized by the donor, to find a particular kind of person to be given money. This is a more unusual bequest and one over which little control can be exercised. However, such a bequest can help persons who otherwise might never have had a chance to develop their skills and talents.

Important criteria for deciding to whom possessions are to be given include: (1) the relationship the donor has with the recipient and the knowledge that the recipient will use the gift to the glory of God; (2) a determination by the donor that the recipient will regard the gift as a challenge; and (3) a feeling of certainty that the gift will not benefit persons or institutions that have only a selfish interest in the donor's possessions.

1. *A giving life pattern is based on glorifying God and treating others as we want to be treated.* This purpose should not be ignored when a gift is given through a will. Recipients ought to be persons who can continue the donor's giving life pattern by using the gift to glorify God and help others. The recipient may be an individual or an institution.

2. *A will ought not include those who are looking for an easier life or financial security.* Jesus warned over and over that once an individual becomes financially secure, his or her values shift subtly. Such individuals tend to become more selfish and protective of what's theirs. Strengthening these negative attitudes through one's will is to negate a life of giving.

A gift through a will must challenge people and institutions. It should give them an opportunity to become something more than they would without it. This means the gift ought to help them increase their witnessing either as individuals or groups. A gift should never relieve a person or a group of their responsibility to continue growing in God's grace.

3. *Many older people find themselves surrounded in their later years by people who try to gain influence and control over them to get at their possessions.* No matter who these people are—a church, an institution, family, or friends—their motives are greedy. They want possessions. When a person feels this is happening, a will is one way of reaching above this selfish inner circle and touching those who are unsuspecting and in need.

This may be illustrated by donation of a body part. The donor usually gives to someone with whom he or she has had no contact. The ministry is carried on by an unsuspecting individual who did not try to manipulate the giver. This type of anonymous gift can be done with other kinds of possessions as well. A will gives a person the opportunity to find a way to reach beyond the greedy with a gift.

How Much Should I Give to Each?

How much to give to each person on the list is never an easy decision. However, it is easier when it is worked at by using percentages rather than actual amounts of money, values of possessions, or possessions. While they have the same effect as figures, percentages relieve a person of the tension and the constant battle for balancing between people and groups that figures seem to demand.

It is relatively easy to divide money by percents. For example, deciding that one-third of the money available after death goes to the church, one-third goes to the family, one-tenth to an organization, 22 percent to a college, and 1 percent to a friend is somehow easier for people than counting out dollars. Relying on percentages makes the distribution of assets following payment of expenses, fees, and taxes that must be taken from an estate upon death much simpler than trying to juggle unrealistic dollar figures.

The important issue is not how much should be given to each person or group but planning the distribution carefully. Only through a plan can a person be certain that what he or she wants to go to whom or what will get there. Once these decisions have been made, computing percentages becomes much simpler.

Some people might feel guilty about distributing their assets through a will in percentages. A giving life pattern is not based on guilt; neither should distribution of possessions at death be guided by it. A giving life pattern is a testimony to God. The will that embodies this attitude continues the testimony in a consistent manner regardless of how the distribution is computed.

Deciding how much to give, whether it is computed as percentages or values, depends on an individual's understanding of the four concepts discussed throughout this book: steward, tithe, first fruits, and jubilee. These are more than words taken from the scriptures; they are guidelines for giving. As such they are important when constructing a will and can assist a person in deciding how much goes to whom or what.

Steward

A will must reflect a person's understanding of being a co-creator with God. When a person dies, the only thing that should be missed is the personal presence, not the influence or continued use of possessions. It is up to the Christian, in facing death and the end of life on earth, to creatively bequeath possessions, including the body, for use to the benefit of God and other humans. Death does not relieve an individual of stewardship responsibilities. It does make planning and careful thought prerequisites. A will ought to be a way to continue being a steward following death.

First Fruits

The idea that a person gives his or her best to glorify God and help others should not be ignored when a will is being written. When the percentages of how much to give to whom and the lists of what to give to whom or what are created, the best of everything is reserved for God's work. The best may be to support people, institutions, or a family. The main ingredient of best means that the tendency for selfishness is curbed, and God's work gets what it requires.

Tithe

As in life, a tithe for God's work is a challenge, not a legal demand. Most people will be able to give much more than a tithe through their will. Endowments that create challenges will probably be much greater than 10 percent of one's possessions. For example, support for a group of dramatists whose aim is performing short and provocative Christian plays in churches might take most of an individual's possessions. Yet the support can be used to sign up new writers, allow the group to expand, and give it a base for operations which can be supplemented by offerings at plays as well as sale of rights to perform.

Even when the resources to be distributed through a will are very limited, the tithe should be a lower limit. It is possible for most people in an affluent society to exist comfortably without needing a financial cushion from

105

others. This should be kept in mind when drawing up a will. A Christian challenges others by giving them something or by not leaving them any monetary support. If the choice is between leaving the money or possessions to those who normally feel they deserve them or giving a tenth of it for God's work, the decision should be the tithe to God.

Jubilee

The most important of the four concepts when writing a will is jubilee. Death can be a time of restitution, of giving back to others what God has blessed us with. This is not to say possessions have been gained illegally or immorally. Most gain in life is due to luck and being in the right place at the right time. While skills and hard work are involved in accumulating things, not everyone who has skills and works hard is blessed with the same luck. It is important to remember this when the will is being drawn.

The aim of jubilee is to re-create a balance among God's people, to level out some of the difference between the haves and the have-nots. It is likely that no one can work out a practical formula that can achieve God's wish for people to share equally with one another. However, it is possible for each person who writes a will to make a strong effort at spreading God's wealth among others rather than trying to make sure it is piled higher within a particular family or group.

At stake in this concept is the giving life pattern. Unless one is willing to practice a form of jubilee, reinstating a form of balance of possessions among people, the giving life pattern is cut short. Using the will as a form of witness to God's intent that people help each other is the only way jubilee can be made a continuation of the giving life pattern.

A Last Word on Willing

Many people feel they don't have enough to bother about writing a will. That isn't so. When you take the time and make the effort to create a giving list, you will be surprised with what you own. Don't allow yourself to think this chapter is written for someone else. It isn't. It includes those who think their only resource is their body. That's enough to help somebody else.

VII

Giving as Commitment

"The other day somebody called the younger generation a 'me first' age group. That's probably a pretty good description, don't you think?"

"If they are, it's because they've had good instruction from us older folks. We are at least partially responsible for helping them develop their basic values."

"Yes, but these people are just selfish! They want everything for themselves. They don't know what sharing or giving means."

"Come to think of it, not many of us give a whole lot. We talk a good game, but when it comes down to what we give and what we keep, our record isn't all that good. The younger generation can't be blamed for the way we've acted."

"You know, George, you're a most distressing person to talk to. You just keep putting blame back on me when I'm trying to put it somewhere else."

"I'm sorry, at least a little bit, Harry. But I am covered with as much blame as you. I don't mean to put you under a cloud of guilt. It's just not fair to make other people scapegoats for our failures."

Sorry to tell you, George, but many people do just that. They are unwilling to take responsibility for their lives. When someone accuses them of not living up to their profession of faith, they say their home situation, environment, psychological state, or any number of other excuses are causes for their failure. They blame everything but themselves.

People are responsible and accountable to God and themselves for their thoughts and actions. No one can relieve them of their shortcomings. No matter how much they protest, they are accountable for what they think, feel, and do.

This is not to deny that life is difficult and God's expectations are severe. Jesus made no excuses for either God's demands or people's frailties. He showed how an individual lives in spite of them. Christian writers and thinkers have continued, following Jesus' death, to interpret to humans both the rigors of existence and the demands of God.

A Christian is an individual who makes a decision to follow Jesus. This decision is life-changing because it gives a person a new set of goals and images after which to model his or her life. In the same way, a decision must be made to start a giving life pattern.

A giving life pattern becomes possible when a person decides to create it. It is not possible until, after the decision to begin it, a second decision is made to develop a disciplined commitment to follow the path wherever it might lead.

The giving life pattern governed Jesus' life. A model of the giving life pattern has survived through the centuries in the teachings of the church. The reason so few have followed that pattern is the effect it has on those who make it their life. It changes people's world view or the way in which they look at themselves, their situations, and how they coexist with others.

In actuality, a giving life pattern is possible only after a person's world view is changed. The change allows an individual to become committed to God's work. Of course, that doesn't mean a person has to run out and become a minister or work full time in the church. Commitment is much deeper than that. It is allowing oneself to be guided by faith which is nurtured by study, discipline, prayer, and action (see chapter 5). It is trusting God to lead and support during hard times. It is being willing to give even when giving doesn't seem possible. It is correcting images of oneself by comparisons with Jesus and others whose lives reflect God's giving pattern.

A giving life pattern is commitment. It is commitment to God, and it brings commitment from God. The life pattern of giving, if one enters into it seriously, becomes a pledge, a contract with God that one's life will reflect God's willingness to give the most precious gift to others. A life committed to God becomes a life in which a person is pledged a new spirit, a new feeling, and a new vision, according to both Jesus and Paul.

The problem with a giving life pattern is that it's different from what people do now. One could be regarded as strange—a person who gives of his or her best, understands that the tithe is a minimum gift, feels that life is an opportunity to be a co-creator with God, and writes a will that incorporates the concept of jubilee. It is a strange set of demands, but Jesus said it wouldn't be a bed of roses. In fact, he warned people that they wouldn't have a place to call their own, that they would be friendless from time to time, and that they would not obey some of the normal social conventions. He also said their reward would be great.

This isn't intended to frighten or discourage people. Far from it. Jesus said that God would give people the strength to live a committed life. No one is asked to carry a burden or chart a course that no one else has carried or traveled. People choosing a giving life pattern will join a host of others who have chosen that pattern before. And God will be with them.

To some people, commitment is a strange concept. They prefer to think life should be free of entanglements, without obligations to tie them down and hinder their activities. These people don't understand life. Each individual's life has to be committed to something or someone. Humans cannot exist as stable beings without a purpose and some goals. Admittedly, the purpose and goals can be very shallow and limited according to what some people do and say. Yet a life needs a stake, a place to which people can tie themselves and return regularly for assurance and motivation. A giving life pattern is one choice among other kinds of commitments that are available to people.

A Christian without a giving life pattern is a contradiction in terms. An individual who has said he or she is committed to Christ—the definition of a Christian—and who has not adopted a giving life pattern is not being true to self or intent. An individual who says, "Christ is my guide," and then refuses to develop a giving life pattern denies—as did Peter when Jesus needed him the most—that God is most important in his or her life.

A giving life pattern is serious business. It is commitment of a person's life, body, and possessions to God. There isn't anything left! Such completeness is hard to come by, but it is expected. Most of us play around at being committed. A giving life pattern means we've stopped playing and are working at being in God's image.

Steward

The steward was a caretaker, a manager in the Old and New Testaments. Applying Jesus' conception of God and humans as partners, the steward becomes a human who is a co-creator with God. The steward is entrusted not only with creation but to be a participant with God in making the creation constructive and helpful.

If an individual is bound closely with God, the dynamics of life are changed. The "me first" idea, instilled in every person as a means of survival, is trained out to become "after you." Such a reversal of roles is impossible without a liberal dose of God's love. No one alone can change his or her life to be in the image of God.

Since it takes a reversal of thought and a changed life pattern to become a steward such as Jesus implied by his life, the need for commitment is evident. Commitment becomes not only trust but discipline. It takes a strong will to stick to the promise a person makes when he or she decides to be committed to God. The intellect and the spirit of the moment are able to say yes to God. It's living that yes every day that is impossible for many people.

There are techniques that make it easier to live that commitment and stay on the road with God. These techniques can help people who want to be stewards to create habits that encourage and reinforce their intent. With practice, habits can make the will stronger.

1. *Worship regularly.* Why make this a point? Because there is worship and then there is worship. Jesus talked about people who like to go to church and sit in the first pews to make a big show of attending. There are some who go just to be seen because, "It's the thing to do." Others attend because it's a habit, and Sunday morning seems a little odd when they don't go. All of these people would say

they are worshiping regularly. Jesus asked for a different kind of worship.

Worship in the way of Jesus means getting in an attitude and atmosphere that make communion with God a reality.[1] Worship redirects daily ways of thinking into channels that allow God to speak and listen to us. Worship is an opportunity to be quiet and wait upon the Lord.

A person who wants to be a co-creator with God must regularly be in touch with God. This can be done through regular prayer and disciplined study which leads to action. There is more to worship, however. It comes from being with others in a common search for God's will and direction. When a person worships, it is with a company of believers. Sharing in worship takes place at a level not found in other ways in life. Regular worship allows an individual to be encouraged and refreshed through the strength of a group.

2. *Think as a steward.* One of the axioms of professional baseball players is that they must always be thinking baseball. It is evident that professional baseball players live in a different environment and have a different world view from most others because the player's conversations are about hitting, fielding, and other things that bore a lot of people. But once they begin talking, it is evident that baseball players think baseball.

A person doesn't suddenly decide he or she is going to think as a steward and it happens. It doesn't happen that way except in very rare situations. Most of us have to try hard and practice daily before we can become proficient at anything, including thinking as a steward. An expert, except for the few I've met who are instant experts on everything, becomes one through practice. It's the same with thinking as a steward. It takes daily practice.

Douglas Hall's book[2] gives insights into the kinds of

113

things a steward can think about. Everything in God's creation is a part of a steward's concern. Thinking as a steward is to feel as a co-creator of everything and everyone. It is to try to change one's perceptions about life and reality. It requires a person to take the blinders of self, culture, and nationality off and to try to think, see, and feel as God or Jesus must feel toward others.

3. *Act as a steward.* One of the advantages of growing older is that a person accumulates experiences. A disadvantage of aging is that many of these experiences are unpleasant. A continuing unpleasant drama is the one in which people "don't want to get involved." Newspapers point out the tragedy of a person being beaten, robbed, or molested while others watch or walk away. It's the story of the man who was finally aided by the good Samaritan in Jesus' parable.

Acting as a steward is to help, to protect, to make it possible for a person or other part of God's creation to make a useful contribution to life. It might mean finding a body organ donor for a desperately ill individual. It might be speaking with someone who has lost a loved one. It might be disciplining an unruly child, young person, or adult. A steward acts as the need occurs, not out of aggression or because he or she is looking for power. The steward acts because he or she knows God cannot intervene unless a human provides the hands, heart, voice, muscle, and brains.

It's so easy to shrug the shoulders and say, "I could have been hit with a lawsuit," to explain not helping someone in need. Most of the time there will be no lawsuit; but even when there might be, the steward is called upon to risk it. God's creation is at stake, and the steward is God's only representative on the scene. Unless the steward acts, God's opportunity to change a life or a situation will have passed unfulfilled.

4. *Practice humility.* A classmate of mine years ago kept saying he had the greatest sermon on humility ever preached. He said it in partial jest, and in doing so captured the spirit of many people whose humility is skin-deep, which means it is a thin veneer. Like all veneers, over time the humility is rubbed off or pulled away and selfishness is exposed for all to see.

Humility is an acceptance of one's abilities, skills, and talents as God-given but used and cultivated by people. No human creates a beautiful voice; it comes with the body. On the other hand, people must study and practice and use a voice before others can appreciate its beauty. Humility recognizes that one shares with God his or her life, talents, and skills. No individual instills in another person innate abilities or desires. Those come from God. How people use and cultivate them is a different story. A steward understands this division of creation and the responsibility he or she assumes with life. That's the reason a steward never thinks too highly of himself or herself.

It is important to have pride in what one is able to do. It is equally important to be proud that God has chosen one to have certain abilities and to give God an adequate amount of the praise. Humility does not mean to deny being able or talented. Humility is acting as a steward, a co-creator with God in this life.

A steward must be committed to God, or he or she will not function effectively. In order to gain the degree of commitment it's going to take, a person interested in being a steward must worship regularly, think and act as a steward, and practice the humility of a co-creator. When these become second nature, a steward will have been

115

created and a giving life pattern will have become a possibility.

First Fruits

Two children were dividing a bag of candy they had just bought. The older of the two was doing the counting.

"One for you, and one for me."

"Jimmy, why do you get all the chocolate ones, and I get the other kind?"

"Oh! Sorry. Here's a chocolate. Now, one for you, and one for me."

"But that's just one. You're still getting all the chocolates."

"It works out that way. Besides, I'm doing the counting."

How typical of people, kids and older folks too! When asked to divide things equally, they always want the bigger half! People's first inclination is to keep what they like the most for themselves. They think up rationalizations for acting that way and convince themselves they are in the right. Unfortunately, their method of dividing their time, energy, gifts, and commitment is no better or just than the children's method with the candy.

It is impossible to give the best of a life without commitment to God. The intellect is a wonderful creation. Training the mind to be understanding, to recognize failings of intent, and honing the conscience to a razor's edge are commendable. As Jesus said, however, unless we give of ourselves, we still haven't committed our lives to God. This was the message to the rich young man as well as to the disciples.

Because giving one's best to God is so difficult, answering some questions each time we're dividing things up to give can help us keep the proper perspective. The answers can indicate the level of commitment as well.

1. *What is the best I have?* Suppose an individual wants to volunteer for service to the church. Does the person respond to a request or tell the pastor or coordinator of volunteers the area in which his or her best might be done? Figuring out what one's best is takes time and effort. Making certain that a part of that best is given for God's work is what the concept of first fruits is about.

Think about your energy. When do you do your most creative, most sustained work? Early morning is the answer of many, but for others it might be early evening or late at night. Everyone has a different internal clock and works best at different times in a day or even in a week. Giving the best to God requires a person to determine when the best occurs and take from that to give to God. For example, if an individual is preparing to lead in the church school, preparing the lesson during the time when he or she is at the most productive energy level is giving of the best. If people are working on a committee, they will ask for assignments that will allow them to work during their peak energy level.

2. *How do I divide the best?* Lives with as many pulls and pushes as most people experience leave them feeling that their best is being demanded in many areas at the same time. Children need attention; work must be accomplished; personal goals have to be met; companions are to be loved; organizations have to be supported; and the list goes on and on. Yet God asks for the best and gets the first share of time, energy, talents, and money.

Jesus said that God wants a person's whole life. That means an individual's life attitude must reflect the commitment to God. A life committed to God will be disciplined in making other commitments. Time will be

117

given carefully so that what is done in organizations and with others reflects the underlying God-centeredness of the life.

3. *How do I know where God wants me to give the best?* An answer to this question should stress *to whom* rather than *where*. God asks for the best to glorify God and to make certain other people are helped and treated well in this life. When these goals are put up front, the givers will make a decision about where their resources can be used to God's greatest glory.

The church, over the years, has been a good place to give one's best because God seems to have worked through it to change people. Other organizations such as colleges; hospitals; institutions for the elderly, mentally incompetent, or emotionally disturbed; and prisons are other places for giving one's best in witness and service. Of course, God needs to be glorified at home, work, recreation, and wherever an individual happens to be. God asks for the best to be given all the time and wherever a person might be.

4. *How much of the best goes to God?* A committed life is one in which everything is dedicated to God. Every waking minute becomes an opportunity to witness and express God's creative force among others. However, people have only so much time, energy, and money. It takes a great deal to exist and to provide for a family. The practical question is, How do I divide my resources so that God does get the best?

The directive of Jesus is to give until we feel it. For some this will mean that the tithe is a challenge, while for others 10 percent is a pittance. Deciding how much is the focus of the next section, which considers the tithe. It is critical to a giving life pattern that a person who is committed to God give of the best, no matter how much that may become.

Tithe

The tithe has had a checkered history moving between a challenge and a legalism. When it becomes a *law* of giving, it loses its challenge and tends to become a hollow legalism which demands a minimum tax from church members. When the tithe is viewed as a challenge, there is a conviction that it is a part of one's commitment to God that underlies the giving life pattern.

One of the most discouraging statements I have encountered came from a minister who said, "I don't give money to the church because my life is committed to it." Somehow he read the Gospel's message of giving in such a way that it didn't ask for his best. The tithe, on the other hand, asks for a part of everything—life, possessions, skills, talents, concern, and everything else—that makes up a person.

The tithe emerges from a committed life; it is not imposed on a Christian. As with everything in life, however, it must be learned. Growing in giving is as important a concept as growing in grace. Tithing is a milepost that can be reached and then passed. It is not a barrier that contains and limits.

Suppose an individual is committing his or her life to God and wants to develop a giving life pattern. The most troublesome part he or she faces is tithing. There are so many financial drains on income and resources that giving a challenging amount seems impossible. How can the person ever get to a tithe, much less pass it? The following steps have helped others and probably can assist this person.

Step 1. *Decide to plan your finances.* Budgeting is a commonly used figure of speech and means many different things. For many households, budgeting is a sterile set of dos and don'ts about money. For others, budgeting is an

119

impractical way of keeping track of resources. The idea of planning finances allows an individual or family to grow or decline in resources and still be able to reflect a life pattern of giving. Making the decision to plan is critical.

Step 2. *Analyze your present life pattern as reflected in your income and expenditures (include savings as expenditures).* The stubs of a checkbook tell more about an individual or family than they care to know. In addition to these data, a tally of the spending money used for a month or more provides a picture of the impulse or free money use.

Step 3. *Decide on percentages to cover major life pattern activities.* Don't worry about meeting some standard. Set the percentages as you realistically believe they meet your life pattern. This means that the percentages you create in this step may vary from those that were computed in step 2 and probably need to vary if you're going to change your life pattern.

Step 4. *Set a percentage for giving that challenges your present pattern but isn't impossible to achieve.* Plan to grow in giving. For example, many people have set a dollar figure for their gifts rather than a percentage. They need to translate the dollars into percentages. If they discover their giving has been 1 percent, they may put the percentage for the next year at 2 or 3 percent. Each year, then, it is possible to move the percentage up.

Step 5. *Review the percentages annually and change them to more accurately reflect your changing life patterns.* A person committed to God is required to make his or her life a witness. This doesn't mean the amount given to the church every year must be an increase. Some years it might be impossible to keep a high percentage of giving to the church because of medical expenses, college costs, or any number of personal necessities. When this happens, the percentages of expenditures change, and giving is expressed in ways other than money. Increased costs for other necessities do not relieve a person with a giving life pattern from continuing to give, although the type of gift may change.

Step 6. *Do not stop with the tithe.* God didn't make the tithe a rule; the church did. It had a history in religious circles and was a convenient measure. God, according to Jesus, asks for much more than the tithe. That's the reason a person with a giving life pattern finds ways to give time, talent, skills, and energy in addition to possessions. It is not enough to give money. Neither is it enough to give 10 percent.

When the tithe becomes a challenge, an individual must be committed to God, or he or she will not develop a giving life pattern. For most people and for most of their adult lives in an affluent society, 10 percent will not be a sufficient gift. It will not reflect either their share of being a co-creator or giving from their best. In an affluent society, a tithe, at best, is a legalism. Yet to a Christian who wants to grow in giving, it can be a challenge. That is the hope it holds for most of us.

Jubilee

Giving is commitment when the concept of jubilee is put into practice through a will or even during a lifetime. The easy way for most people to dispose of their possessions after death is to let others worry about it. This is a shortsighted and selfish end to a life. It is shortsighted because it doesn't recognize the opportunities that death provides to a person who wants to distribute possessions. It is selfish because an individual doesn't want to be bothered with planning something which won't benefit him or her.

121

If a Christian has learned about the message of Christ and put that together with jubilee, giving beyond death is not left to others. Careful attention is given to finding out how much possessions are worth, who or what would most benefit from them, and the best method for making certain these persons or groups receive the possessions. A person committed to God will embrace jubilee as a way of expressing the giving life pattern after death.

A Last Word

Once people have become committed to God through Jesus, their way of living is changed. Their lives take on a new reflectiveness based on God's love and giving pattern. They discover they are stewards or co-creators in the world with God, not just transitory inhabitants of a strange environment.

They discover also that giving is a primary activity for them. They give of their best and use the tithe as a challenge against which to measure their contributions of time, energy, skills, talents, and money. Their giving doesn't stop at death but extends beyond through a will that gives possessions and body parts to others. They share wealth rather than accumulate it.

Notes

I. Old Testament Basis of Giving

1. Robert H. Pfeiffer, *Introduction to the Old Testament*, rev. ed. (New York: Harper & Brothers, 1948), pp. 3-10.
2. Douglas John Hall, *The Steward* (New York: Friendship Press [for the Commission on Stewardship of the National Council of Churches], 1982), pp. 17-19.

II. New Testament Interpretations

1. Manfred Holck, Jr., *Money and Your Church* (New Canaan, Conn.: Keats Publishing, 1974), pp. 50-51.
2. Luther P. Powell, *Money and the Church* (New York: Association Press, 1962), p. 16.
3. George A. Buttrick, ed., *Interpreter's Dictionary of the Bible* (Nashville: Abingdon Press, 1962), vol. 3, pp. 1001-2.

III. The Church and Giving

1. Williston Walker, *A History of the Christian Church* (New York: Charles Scribner's Sons, 1918).
2. John Knox, "The Ministry in the Primitive Church," *The Ministry in Historical Perspectives*, ed. H. Richard Niebuhr and Daniel D. Williams (New York: Harper & Brothers, 1956), pp. 1-26.
3. Powell, *Money and the Church*, p. 24.
4. Ibid., pp. 25-26.
5. Ibid., pp. 26 ff.
6. Ibid., p. 30.
7. Ibid., p. 33.

8. Ibid., pp. 32-52.
9. Ibid., pp. 68 ff.
10. George A. E. Salstrand, *The Story of Stewardship in the United States of America* (Grand Rapids: Baker Book House, 1956), pp. 13-14. See also Powell, pp. 85 ff.
11. Salstrand, pp.15-17.
12. Powell, p. 136.
13. Ibid., p. 135.
14. Salstrand, pp. 31-39.
15. Ibid., pp. 41-46.
16. Powell, pp. 151-72.
17. Salstrand, pp. 41-46.
18. John Naisbitt, *Megatrends: Ten New Directions Transforming Our Lives* (New York: Warner Books, 1982), pp. 11-38.
19. Powell, pp. 85-103.
20. Ibid., p. 123.
21. Salstrand, pp. 41-46.
22. Powell, p. 173.
23. Salstrand, pp. 41-46.
24. Hall, *The Steward*. The entire book pushes toward this concept.

IV. Giving in a Time of Affluence

1. Willis W. Harman, *An Incomplete Guide to the Future,* (San Francisco: San Francisco Book Co., 1976), especially chapter 5. See also Naisbitt, *Megatrends: Ten New Directions Transforming Our Lives,* as well as Alvin Toffler, *The Third Wave* (New York: Bantam Books, 1980).
2. Max Weber, *The Protestant Ethic and the Spirit of Capitalism* (New York: Charles Scribner's Sons, 1958).
3. Ibid.
4. Naisbitt, *Megatrends: Ten New Directions Transforming Our Lives.*

V. Giving as a Life Pattern

1. Arnold Mitchell, "Life Ways, Futures, and Markets," undated research report. (Menlo Park, Calif.: Stanford Research Institute. The paper was developed in 1975.)
2. Powell, *Money and the Church,* p. 92n.
3. Holck, *Money and Your Church,* pp. 22 ff..
4. There are several books on individual giving, but one is especially useful: Martin E. Carlson, *Why People Give* (New York: Council Press [National Council of Churches], 1968).
5. All denominations as well as several independent publishing houses have these kinds of materials. One model used by several denominations is called *Commpac.* It is based on intensive research

and evaluation of programs over several years. It is available through denominational stewardship offices or the Commission on Stewardship, National Council of Churches, 475 Riverside Drive, Room 830, New York, N.Y. 10115.

VI. Giving Through Willing

1. For an older statistic see Douglas W. Johnson and George C. Cornell, *Punctured Preconceptions* (New York: Friendship Press, 1972), pp. 156. A newer, though much more limited statistic is in Douglas W. Johnson, "Survey of Church Member Experiences and Opinions About Death Education, Funeral Preplanning and Funeral Practices" (1980). This study is available through the Family Life Section of the National Council of Churches.
2. Powell, *Money and the Church*, especially chapter 5.

VII. Giving as Commitment

1. Evelyn Underhill, *Worship* (New York: Harper & Brothers, 1936), pp. 15 ff.
2. Hall, *The Steward*.